i am...

The 90-Day Journey To Loving Yourself For Who You Are

sandy lynn

acknowledgments

I would never have been able to write this book without the encouragement of my beautiful Mother, Sirkka Kainulainen. Mom, we talked about this book so many times and I'm so sorry that I didn't finish it before you left this physical world, but I have felt you with me every step of the way. I love you. To my dad, Bob Start, I don't think either one of us realized how much I actually learned from you. I am so grateful that we were able to connect in this life and do some healing together, even if we started a little late. I will see you on the other side.

I am so grateful for Ken Stewart, my partner of 20 years. Even though our marriage didn't make it for the long run and we had so many ups and downs, I am so blessed to have had you in my life. We taught each other so many things, and we brought two beautiful children into this world. There was a time when this was a dream for both of us, and in the moments that I questioned myself I could hear you telling me not to give up. We lost you much too soon and you are sorely missed. To my children, Ben and Riley, you are my reason, my everything, and I love you both more than words can ever say.

I would also like to thank the many people who encouraged and taught me throughout this whole process. Jay Bradley, my friend and mentor, bless you for believing in me even when I didn't. Ellie Shoja, you have been more than a writing coach, you have become a friend. I send so much love and gratitude to you both! Alexandre Venancio and Dana Goldstein, who designed the cover and the inside of the book, thank you for your suggestions and support. As a first-time author your patience was so much needed and appreciated.

Finally, thank you to all of the friends and family members who listened, let me bounce ideas off of them, proofread, edited, and just generally put up with my little meltdowns throughout this process…I am so grateful to you all!

dedication

To all who inspired me to raise my voice and love myself the way I AM. I love you all so much.
To those who inspired me to write it but will probably never read it. I forgive you, and I send you love.
And finally, to the readers. May this book bring you the same feeling of peace and accomplishment that I felt when I finished writing it.
I see you, and I love you...for WHO YOU ARE!

NOT

You are not your age,
Nor the size of clothes you wear,
You are not a weight,
Or the color of your hair.

You are not your name,
Or the dimples in your cheeks,
You are all the books you read,
And all the words you speak.

You are your croaky morning voice,
And the smiles you try to hide,
You're the sweetness in your laughter,
And every tear you've cried.

You're the songs you sing so loudly,
When you know you're all alone,
You're the places that you've been to,
And the one that you call home.

You're the things that you believe in,
And the people that you love,
You're the photos in your bedroom,
And the future you dream of.

You're made of so much beauty,
But it seems that you forgot,
When you decided that you were defined,
By all the things you're not.

Erin Hanson

foreword

I met Sandy over 35 years ago at summer camp. We enjoyed some nice times together during our stay, but we lost touch for decades afterward. We reconnected just a few years ago over the power of Breathwork healing. I had the honor to work with Sandy and to support her on her personal transformation journey.

I've told Sandy from day one that she is very powerful and it's rare for me to work with somebody like her. She's intuitive, energetically aligned, and tapped into a higher power that most of us cannot seem to access. And like many of us, she spent many years struggling to see herself fully. I've been a witness to her growth and tremendous healing over many years, and it's been a joy to share this work with somebody who has now become a dear friend.

This book brings to light the most important theme of our lives; learning to fully love and accept ourselves. This topic has been a long and challenging one for me, and I only wish that somebody had written this book years ago when I needed it the most.

The good news is that change is absolutely possible! No

Foreword

matter where you're at, what you've been through, or how long it's taken, everything happens for a reason and all in Divine timing…you are always being guided.

This book has shown up for you at the perfect time in your life. Create the space to fully dive in and follow Sandy's wise words and intuitive journal prompts so that you can fast track your own growth. You truly deserve to enjoy more self-love, self-acceptance, nurturing, and happiness, and this book will ignite it all.

While deep healing is not always easy, I can't think of anything more important than you being the most authentic and loving version of you. So, read on and discover who YOU ARE!

Happy healing.

Love, Jay Bradley

introduction

Why This Book Is Important

Do you feel that you are attractive? Think hard about this question and be truly honest with yourself. If you had the opportunity, would you change anything about your appearance? I believe that everyone has at least one thing they would change if they had the chance. I have struggled with my weight for most of my life. The funny thing is that even during the times when I was happy with my weight there were other things that I was self-conscious about. I was very well-endowed and I remember having talks with my friends about 'boob size'. They all wished that they had bigger boobs. I had what they wanted and I wished that mine were smaller. Where does this come from? Why do we do this to ourselves? It seems that no matter what body size we are, what gender, what age, we are always striving to be 'better'. We are not content with ourselves. We cannot see the special and unique beauty that we all possess.

We live in what I like to call a culture of criticism. This is a

Introduction

society that focuses on the negative and sets standards for beauty that are almost impossible for the average person to live up to. According to the Centers for Disease Control and Prevention, "the average waist size of a woman in the United States is 38.7 inches...the average weight for a woman is around 170 pounds." This means that on average, the American woman is a size 18-20 (Holland, 2019). Yet, our media is plastered with models who are more often than not displaying the 'ideal' measurements of 36-24-36 (bust, waist, hips) or what's more commonly known as the 90-60-90 rule. It is no wonder that we are all so hard on ourselves and have difficulty loving ourselves. This lack of self-love trickles out and adds to a world that is already filled with so much disconnection.

So we have this culture of criticism, a world full of disconnected people, and along with that we have become an 'Eeyore' society. (For those of you who do not know who Eeyore is, he is a character in Winnie the Pooh books who is described as pessimistic and depressed). Everyone automatically focuses on the negative. For example, I have a TikTok account. I don't post a lot but when I do it's always positive and my videos have a healing vibe. I am thrilled when I can get a few 'likes' and comments because it means that I have touched that person in a positive way. I have an acquaintance that also has a TikTok account. His entire account is full of negative videos, mostly bashing our prime minister; videos talking about how horrible the government is and how our lives are going to shit. Then I look at the comments and the likes on his videos. His videos receive at least 10 times more interactions than mine do. It's as though people are just feeding off of other people's negativity. We can feel the vibrations around us become lower and lower, more and more negative; and instead of fighting it we just let it suck us into the black hole of despair.

Introduction

For people who are trying to make any kind of change in their physical, spiritual or mental health, this is extremely discouraging. I don't know how many videos I've seen of individuals who do not meet this society's standards for the 'perfect' body being belittled, teased and patronized while at the gym. It's situations like this that show you where the mindset of our country and our culture is at this moment in time. It is no wonder that so many people struggle with self rejection and self hatred and self criticism. It's almost impossible to keep up with what our society expects us to look like. When I was younger, women weren't supposed to have big butts. It was supposed to be small and tight and firm. Now, women get butt implants. I go into my dance class and these young women wear little booty shorts, and their butts are so jiggly and they're so proud of that. Back in the day I used to be so proud of my perfectly shaped tight ass. Now I'm almost ashamed of it because it's not as large and wiggly and jiggly as it should be. How the hell does that happen? And why is it ok?

Speaking of shame, let's talk about that for a minute. Shame is a complicated emotion. It comes in so many different forms. It's also one of those hard emotions to deal with because we don't talk about it....because we're ashamed to, of course. So we are all walking around with some sort of shame inside but we are not helping each other to heal because we don't want anyone else to know what it is that we are ashamed of. It's a vicious circle. In my case, as with many women, much of my shame stems from body issues. Or does it? If we explore this a little bit further, we can see it goes much deeper than that.

I developed at a very early age. My mother noticed that I was holding my breasts when I was running and decided it was time for me to get a bra. Actually, she literally *whispered* to me that it was time to go bra shopping and I wasn't sure as to why it was such a secretive thing. I was 9 years old. When I did start wearing a bra I was teased mercilessly about my 'big boobs' and my back was always red from having the strap snapped. The boys would dare each other to try and get in a squeeze. I started to realize that it didn't matter what I wore, it would always be revealing unless it was heavy and baggy. And those large breasts stuck out like beacons, even when I didn't want them to. When I think back, it was around this time that I adopted the stance of crossing my arms over my chest. To this day my posture is terrible because I was always hunching my shoulders trying to keep my chest from sticking out too much.

By the time I was 11 I had my period, and it was made very clear to me that I could now get pregnant. It was never really discussed, however, *how* I could get pregnant. Sex was something that my mother never talked about, and I could never ask questions about it because the simple answer was that <u>you just didn't do it</u>. Everything I learned about sex (other than it was bad) I learned at school, or through my friends who seemed to know much more than I did. So…imagine being a 12 year-old girl who could easily pass for a young woman, but has no clue about sex. The attention from older men was confusing as it both intrigued and embarrassed me. Also confusing was the way other girls and women treated me at times. I was often branded a flirt or a slut, even though I was rather shy and a virgin.

The messages from my mother stuck with me however, and I held onto my virginity longer than most of my friends did. And then I got teased about that. I believed my mother when she told me that if a boy really loved me he would wait. So I dated a few boys and never gave in to their pleading. And then, I fell in love for the very first time. He was perfect, we were perfect, everything was perfect because he loved me too and we were going to be together forever; until we weren't. He loved me, but I refused to have sex and he couldn't wait, so he left. I was destroyed. After that I didn't care. I slept with the very next boy that I dated because in my mind it didn't matter anymore. Either you gave in, or you got used to being alone. Add to this a low self esteem and 'daddy issues' (my dad abandoned the family when I was 7, but that's another story) and I was pretty easy prey.

So...I was ashamed of my developing body. I was ashamed of the attention I was getting. I was ashamed of myself for enjoying the attention. I was ashamed for not having sex, then I was ashamed for having sex. And I turned all of this into a hatred for my own body. It didn't matter whether I was slim or heavy. It didn't matter how beautiful other people told me I looked. It didn't matter how many things I accomplished or how nice of a person I was. When I looked in the mirror all I saw were my physical flaws. At one point in my life, due to health issues, I had lost an extreme amount of weight. My skin was dry and my hair was falling out due to being malnourished. I look back at photos now and realize that I looked sickly and I was basically skin and bones. But at the time, in my reflection I still saw the chubby girl with the big boobs and bad posture looking back at me.

These issues stuck with me for most of my life. In my younger years all I wanted was affection. Sex was just something that had to be done. It wasn't enjoyed, it was a chore—a trade-off. Always hoping that just once, I would mean more to someone than just a chance to "get lucky". As I got older and had more serious relationships, sex became an issue because I was so 'uptight'. I had been taught that sex was shameful and should be done when necessary but not talked about. That caused a lot of problems because I could never relax and my partners felt like I was impossible to *'please'*. I was with a man for 20 years and

Introduction

right up until the end of our relationship I had to have the lights turned off before I got undressed for bed.

It took me 50 years to figure out what exactly I was ashamed of and where this shame came from. We talk about young females and their body issues and photoshop and the images and advertisements that our society reigns down upon their young, impressionable minds. But do we ever really look at the depths of these issues? My shame stemmed from before I was born. From my mother having to face the shame of getting pregnant at 17 at a time when this was unacceptable. From my prim and proper paternal grandmother and her shame in knowing that her son had gotten a girl pregnant, and had to have a shotgun wedding. On top of that he then ran away from his responsibilities. I was the result of that pregnancy, and I always felt resentment from her. I never felt fully accepted by my dad's side of the family. The shame I felt growing up without a father, and having it pointed out to me often, especially at school. More shame from my mother as I got older and she taught me to hide my body, probably trying to make sure that I didn't end up in the same situation that she did. The body issues I had (and still sometimes have) are what I call *'surface shame'*; and *'surface shame'* is a by-product of years…sometimes generations of inner wounds that have never been healed.

We can never be sure where the shame stems from for each and every individual, but we can help them discover what the roots of that shame are. Yes, for a lot of young women (and men) it comes out as body issues. And yes, the way that our society portrays male and female 'roles' in the media continues to magnify the situation. I can only tell my story from a woman's perspective, but men are living with shame as well. Men are taught not to show emotion, don't cry, only weaklings have mental health issues. They are often shamed when they seek any kind of support or treatment. But if we want to fix this, changing our advertisements and societal views would only be the beginning.

I believe that those of us who have discovered the value of healing must bring more attention to it. We need to both nurture our own souls and support each other in that healing process. We must believe, and teach our children to believe, that loving oneself is not selfish…it is selfless. We need to teach future generations the importance of valuing ourselves so that we can value each other. We need to build a foundation on the premise that value comes from within, not from what society or the media tells us is valuable. *It is only by talking about our shame that we will no longer be ashamed of it.*

It's Not Just About Women And It's Not Just About Weight

Societal views of perfection have a huge impact on the way we view our bodies. It's interesting to note the standard of beauty has shifted over history. In the past, being skinny and tan used to mean you're poor, malnourished, and you work in the fields. Whereas wealthier people had pale skin and a bit more meat on their bones because they had access to food and healthcare and could hire people to do the physical labour. During the 70's and 80's we saw the advancement in the reach of the media. We saw stick thin supermodels like Twiggy. We had the introduction of music videos in which, more often than not, the main focus was slender women with large breasts and next to nothing for clothing on. We have seen some changes in recent years with the introduction of plus size models. But even the plus size models have perfect proportions: large busts and large hips and ass,

Introduction

which makes their waists look smaller. The strive for perfection has left not just women, but everyone, in a situation where they're never 100% satisfied with how they look.

For example, Steve is a 6'2" successful, handsome, funny guy. He is 50 years old, born Canadian, but currently living in LA. When Steve talks about dating, his belief is that he has to be really fit in order to date his dream girl. From his viewpoint, no girl is going to want to be with him if he's chubby, so when he feels fat he tends to take a break from dating. Who is Steve's dream girl? She's in her late 30's, takes care of herself, and is slender and fit. Basically society's image of the perfect girl. So not only is Steve missing out on some really great women by only wanting to date women that meet society's standards, he is also selling himself really short. He's ignoring all of the wonderful traits and assets that he has to offer by judging himself (and his future girlfriend) solely on physical appearance. Then there's Paul. Paul is In his mid-40s. He is successful, super sweet, kind, generous, and a bit 'nerdy'. Paul hates the way he looks and he believes that he will never be loved because he's not handsome enough. He struggles with asking women out because he has such a strong fear of rejection. When Paul was encouraged to practice looking in the mirror and finding something about his body and himself that he loves, his eyes filled with tears. These men are not the exception.

Sad but true statistics:

- **85%** of women do not consider themselves to be attractive…
- More than half of women don't believe other people like them

- Only **1 in 5** women feels confident in their appearance.
- **61% of adults** said they either felt negative or very negative about their body image most of the time. A further **66% of children felt the same way.**
- Around 80% of people between the ages of 33 and 54 don't feel confident in their appearance
- **90% of people over the age of 45** said they don't consider themselves to be attractive.
- **Only 13%** of women said they were body positive
- **Approximately 94%** of teen girls have been shamed for their body shape or size in the past

20 Self Esteem Statistics That Will Help You Feel Better (2023)

Our current society is almost designed so that no one will ever truly 'fit in'. It's not a wonder that so many young girls suffer from eating disorders, or that nearly everyone I meet has suffered from some kind of anxiety disorder. It's so evident even in the television programs that are so popular today. Programs like, *The Real Housewives of Beverly Hills*, where beautiful women have all of the money in the world but they are still unsatisfied and self-conscious. Women that the rest of us see as absolutely beautiful are constantly running for botox or plastic surgery, altering their bodies in order to live up to the expectation placed upon them. This dissatisfaction is a strong indication that the problem runs much deeper than just physical looks. There's a piece inside of so many of us that is broken and bruised. The body is just the container for what's on the inside. Like the analogy of the apple, the skin might be perfect and red and shiny, but there could be large bruises just under the surface. Imagine how good it would feel to mend our relation-

Introduction

ships with ourselves, to fix the bruises on the inside, so that we can truly be in love with who we are, no matter what we look like.

What's In It For You?

Let me ask you a question.
Do you love yourself? I mean really, truly love yourself?

I believe that we all like to think that we do. Especially those of us who have been on a healing journey. But if we are talking in terms of Unconditional Love, how many of us can say that we love ourselves *unconditionally*? When we think of our love for the people around us it's a lot easier to talk about unconditional love. We love that person freely and completely, with no strings attached. We love that person whether they are short or tall, big or small. Our love is not based on what they can do for us or how they can help us. We just love them, no matter what. But how many of us can say that we love ourselves the same way? When it really comes down to it, can you look in the mirror and honestly say, "I love every part of me?"

To be totally honest, truly loving myself is something that I am constantly working on. I have to work on it every day. My story is similar to many others. I had an unhappy childhood, an absent father, and I struggled with my relationship with my mother. I developed at a very young age and was receiving attention from men, which was both enjoyable and confusing at the same time. I had big boobs and hips, which the boys loved me for and the girls hated me for. I was a bigger boned, curvy girl at a time when the ideal woman was a size zero. I wasn't fat, but I wasn't super model skinny, and that's what mattered. Especially because my mom and my sister were stick thin, and I was often compared to them. People don't realize how their 'harmless' comments about a young girl's body can cause so much damage.

Because of the way I felt about myself and my body, I became a shadow of what I should have been. I was a people pleaser, a 'yes' woman. I would bend over backwards and give the shirt off my back to anyone who needed it without a thought for myself. I put myself last. When I got into relationships I allowed myself to be taken advantage of, to be spoken down to, and to be mistreated. Like so many, I found comfort in food. Like so many, I had gotten bored during the pandemic, and I put on weight. Like so many, I had been through a brutal relationship with a narcissist who contributed to my low self esteem, and I put on weight. Like so many, I had suffered through grief and other stressful situations, and I put on weight. I finally got to a point where I felt I didn't recognize myself. Going out of the house was a stressful situation because I put on outfit after outfit; only to look in the mirror and chastise myself and then throw it on the floor and try something else. I was ashamed of the way I looked and I didn't want anyone else to see me like that. I couldn't see the beauty that was inside of me.

I have been on a journey of healing and self-discovery…and I have been on that journey for a few years now. I have worked with my Inner Child on healing past trauma, and dealt with ancestral wounds. The main hurdle that kept coming up for me was my self confidence and self esteem. These were issues that I had worked on time and time again but they still kept getting in the way. The most frustrating thing was that I knew where these issues stemmed from and why I carried them, but I couldn't seem to change them. I was a teacher, a public speaker, and people seemed to love being around me but I still could not feel my inner strength and have confidence in my ability as a healer. The funniest thing about this was that I was helping people all the time; they told me so. I knew what to say and how to say it. I knew how to guide them. I knew how to use my training in holistic healing to make them feel better. The saddest thing about this was that I could not seem to apply these same words, guidance and abilities to myself.

Of course, I was blind to the way I saw myself. I just kept telling myself: "I'm good, I'm healing. I'm learning how to love myself." But I was still ashamed of the way my body looked. And then one day someone asked me: "Sandy, do you love yourself?" I thought I had the answer all figured out. "Absolutely I love myself! I love who I am. I have a great personality. I make people laugh. I am a powerful healer and I love to guide and support others to heal themselves." I added that I believed that I could love myself without loving my physical body. But I was confronted with another question: Can you really accept yourself and be your authentic self if you can't accept your body? And then I started to think about how there is a connection between my relationship with my body and my relationship with my inner self.

This was really brought to my attention one day when I was looking at photos of myself. I was preparing to present a workshop and the organization I was presenting for asked for a bio with a photo to put in their brochure. Anyone who knows me well knows that I have never liked having my picture taken. I can truly say that of all the pictures that have been taken of me over the years, there are probably about half a dozen in which I actually like the way I look. So, I started to ask myself if there was any connection to how I was feeling about myself at the time, both mentally and physically. The funny thing was that in some of those photos I was heavier than others, in some of them I was younger, and in some of them I was older. The common denominator was that I was feeling good inside as well as outside.

Uncovering this made me very sad when I realized how few of these photos there actually were.

The next thing I dove into were the photos of myself that I absolutely hated. There were a lot of those. The one I remember most distinctly was taken at a family wedding. I was a bit heavier than I would have liked and I wasn't extremely happy with my body shape, but I spent many hours shopping for and trying on dresses. I finally found one that I felt great in! I bought shoes, a handbag and jewelry to coordinate. I spent a lot of time on my hair and makeup. I listened to so many people tell me how good I looked. And then something happened at the wedding that had nothing to do with my appearance but made me feel very unappreciated and taken for granted. It tore at my self-confidence and made me question myself. When I saw the pictures the next day I hated them. All I could see was how fat and old I looked. I couldn't stand the fact that other people had seen me looking like that and it had been recorded for all eternity. And I had never made the connection between how I felt about myself internally and how I felt about my physical appearance until that moment.

I think now, that if anyone was to ask again: "Can you truly love yourself without loving your physical body?" I would answer differently. I think that body acceptance and self-love are two different things, but they are directly related and directly affect one another. The way you feel about your physical body has an impact on your self-esteem and self-confidence, and it's hard to feel true self-love when those aspects of yourself are damaged. This is very interesting to me, because with all of the healing I have done, I feel like the final hurdle I have to jump is directly related to my belief in myself…which is, in essence, my self-esteem (or lack thereof). For many years I've been feeling like I've been taking one step forward, then two steps back. I've never been able to pull myself completely 'out of the rut'. I keep

Introduction

slipping back in. I'm thinking now that this might be because I have never learned to accept and love my physical body for what it is. That, in turn, affects every other aspect of how I feel about my whole self. It's like the difference between loving yourself and loving yourself *unconditionally*. This was going to be my hardest battle, but I also knew that it would be the final battle to finally reach inner peace.

So I ask you now, to ask yourself: How are you going to show up fully in the world if you can't come home to your own body?. Does loving yourself unconditionally mean that you should be okay with being overweight or unhealthy? No. But it does mean that you should learn to be more accepting of the part of yourself that makes mistakes; or eats that piece of chocolate. It means that you should change the way you talk to yourself in your head. It means that you will not beat yourself up if you miss a day of working out because you got too busy. It also means that as you start loving yourself *unconditionally,* you will start taking better care of your physical body; and you won't keep slipping back into the rut. This book is about finding out who you really are underneath all of the pain and the hurt and the insecurities. Discovering who you are at your very core, and loving that person unconditionally. It's about being able to say: "I AM WORTHY, I AM LOVED, I AM ENOUGH!"

It is so important that you know that you are not alone in this experience. When I started to talk about my journey with others, I realized very quickly that almost everyone is struggling with something. We need to talk about these things; support each other through them. I am going to be the first one to say that it isn't always easy, sometimes I felt like I was taking two steps forward and one step back, but it sure has been worth it! I have accomplished things that I have been dreaming about for years but haven't had the confidence to tackle. I used to feel like I had a 50 pound weight on my chest all of the time, but the more I learn and the more I heal, the lighter I feel. I have come to a place of peace and I feel content, satisfied and grateful most days. I hope that by sharing my stories and struggles I can inspire you to recognize the amazing and beautiful soul that you are. Show yourself some grace. Seize this opportunity! I look forward to sharing this difficult but beautiful journey with you.

how to get the most out of this book

Prepare to Give Yourself Some **'HUGS'**

They say it takes 90 days to create a new habit or break an old one. So I have organized this book into 4 easy steps:

- Step 1: **H**onoring Where You Are At Right Now (1 week)
- Step 2: **U**nlearning the Past (4 weeks)
- Step 3: **G**ive Yourself some Credit (4 weeks)
- Step 4: **S**elf Gratitude! (4 weeks)

My goal for you over the next 90 days (technically 91 days/13 weeks) is for you to learn to give yourself some **HUGS!**
The 13 Week Plan

- *Weekly Layout:* Each week will have a theme, a weekly meditation, a weekly challenge, and daily affirmations and exercises.

- *Journal Exercises:* You can complete the exercises right in the book. Another suggestion is to use a blank journal in case you want to expand on any of the entries. This will allow you to save the book and go through it again at a later date just to remind yourself how important you are!
- *Quotes:* I love quotes! Each week will start with an inspirational quote that fits what we are working on for the next 7 days. If you love quotes too, think about hanging a white board on the wall in your bedroom that you can write inspirational quotes on. It will be the first thing you see when you wake up, so you will always start your day on a positive note! You can also use a sheet of plain paper or whatever you have handy and tape it to the wall, the mirror, or anywhere where it will be very visible to you.
- *Daily Affirmations:* Throughout this book you will see suggested Daily Affirmations. Affirmations are a way of helping your mind to replace negative thoughts with positive ones. Repeating positive affirmations daily helps to create new pathways within your brain. This makes it easier to adopt new and empowering thoughts and beliefs. Affirmations should always be specific and in the present tense. For example, "My business IS successful" rather than, "My business WILL BE successful." Keep them short and sweet so you can remember them, and make sure that they coincide with your goals and values. When using affirmations, consistency is the key. Choose a time each day, preferably upon waking or just before bed, and repeat your affirmations. You can even

create your own little ritual such as lighting a candle or burning palo santo or sage. Make it a habit; make it your own. I suggest writing the daily affirmations on your white board or paper, and each day when you repeat the new affirmation, include the ones from the days before so that at the end of the week you will say all 7. I also feel that affirmations have much more impact when you say them out loud. You might also want to write them on a little card or piece of paper to carry with you and repeat throughout the day.

- *Weekly Meditations:* A meditation session has been created for each week, based on the weekly theme. The recordings of these meditations can be accessed through my website www.breathehealingcentre.com. Just click on the MENU and you will see a page entitled 'I Am'. When you get to that page, simply scroll down and click on the title of the meditation recording for that week.

Some Notes On Meditation:

A lot of people get overwhelmed when they hear the word meditation. Please don't overthink it. There are so many different ways to work on being 'present'. Start with simple things and work your way up. You can start by just being present doing everyday things. For example, when you're eating something: sit quietly, take small bites, notice the feeling in your mouth, the texture, the taste. Notice how you're chewing and swallowing. You can even do this with just a raisin or a piece of chocolate and write about it in your journal. This can be done during almost any activity. You can take a mindful walk or shower. When you start meditating, it is important to note that consistency is more important than length. It's better to meditate for five minutes every day than for 30 minutes once a week. Set the scene: set up your space for comfort with pillows, a blanket in case you feel chilly, light a candle, burn some sage or some palo santo. For the Weekly Meditation in this book I have started out with shorter meditation times and we will work our way up as we go.

step 1: honor where you are

"The curious paradox is that when I accept myself just as I am, then I can change."
Carl Rogers

WE ALREADY KNOW that everything that we have experienced in our lives to this point has shaped us into who we are. The things said and done to us, with us, and around us have molded our personalities, the way we treat others, and the way we treat ourselves. Our negative life experiences are our *personal* trauma. This is the trauma that we are aware of, for the most part. But we can also suffer from *generational* trauma. Your emotions develop and are, ultimately, a part of you long before you are born. Women form and carry eggs when they are a fetus, so at one time, a part of you was actually within your grandmother's body. This also means that, in a way, this part of you was exposed to your grandmother's emotions and experiences. Along with any physical family traits, we can also carry the stories of our ancestors, which can be a proud and wonderful thing. But if we carry forward any conflict or unresolved issues, this can become the *generational* trauma that we are (for the most part) *unaware* of.

Whether *personal* or *generational*, we need to become aware of how our trauma has affected us. We cannot fix it or heal it until we know what it is and what it's doing. This whole first week is going to be about becoming more aware of exactly how it is that we feel about ourselves. Most times we don't really have any idea how deep our negative feelings go, or we don't think of them as negative feelings because we disguise them as humor. In my case, for example, I didn't realize it until one of my friends pointed it out. I had referred to myself as an 'old, fat broad'. I didn't think anything of it until it was brought to my attention that I was using self deprecating humor to protect myself. I would make fun of myself before anyone else could.

Throughout this journey you must be prepared to be truly honest with yourself and look at your life through someone else's eyes. For me, journaling was a huge thing. (Hence, this book). I just randomly wrote down everything that came to mind. I didn't think about it, I didn't judge it, I just wrote it down. I filled pages and pages with memories from my childhood. My seemingly 'normal' childhood. And then I sat down and read them all. But when I read them I tried to read them as if I were reading my best friend's journal. I asked myself: "How would I feel about these stories if they weren't about me? What emotions would come through for me if my best friend were telling me about these things that had happened to her?" When I was able to see it from another perspective, I had a 'holy shit!' moment. This person I was reading about had been through a lot of pain and unfairness in her life…and for the first time it hit me that this person was me.

This week is all about realizing where you are at as far as how you feel about yourself. It is so important that you go deep inside and complete the exercises with complete honesty. You might be surprised at what comes up for you. It may be an emotional experience but don't hold back. You have to feel it to heal it. And it will be worth it, I promise!

Much luv, Sandy

week 1: knowing where i am

"The most powerful relationship you will ever have is the relationship with yourself."
Steve Maraboli

IN ORDER TO MOVE FORWARD, we must first acknowledge where we are currently at. Sometimes this is difficult because it requires taking a very good, honest look at yourself as if you were looking in from the outside. Do you, or can you, recognize the parts of you that are unhealed? It is important that you are prepared to go deep under the surface and lift off the mask that you show to the rest of the world. You may find out things about yourself that you weren't even aware of.

For me, this first step was very eye opening. I learned things about myself that I really needed to. I also learned things that I didn't really want to learn but had to. For example, I had always thought of myself as the 'go to' girl, the savior, the healer, and I was proud of that. But there came a point when I had to realize that sometimes I was more like a doormat. I wasn't the 'go to' girl, I was the 'yes' girl. Everybody came to me because they knew I wouldn't say no. I carried so much guilt inside of me because of my childhood experiences, and my self esteem was so low, that I didn't realize when people were taking advantage of me. And it wasn't necessarily that they did it purposely or maliciously. They were just so used to me being there to take care of everything.

I used to be so proud of how strong I was. Nothing phased me…I never broke down; I just kept on going. I knew what had to be done and who needed to be taken care of and I did it. There was no point in crying…emotions showed weakness. When someone "screwed me over" I didn't get angry. I didn't see the point in getting angry, it didn't solve anything. Most of the time if I did get angry it was because I was angry with myself. What had *I* done to *make* that person "screw me over"? How could I be so stupid as to let it happen? And then finally I realized that I was never going to be truly happy until I peeled away all of those layers of who *other people wanted me to be* and found the person that *I wanted to be.*

So, before we get started, you need to relax and open yourself up to really experiencing this journey. Relax your tongue, unclench your sphincter, drop your shoulders, unclench your jaw and create a space between your teeth. I'll bet you didn't even realize you were doing any of these things. Release the stress and continue reading. I'll be here, you're not alone.

Weekly Challenge: Be brutally honest with yourself when completing all of the journal entries and exercises for this week.

Weekly Meditation: Week 1–Knowing Where I Am

day 1: how do you feel about you?

TODAY'S AFFIRMATION: *I deserve to feel loved, and to enjoy my life.*

I THINK a lot of us kind of lost our way during the pandemic. Even when quarantine was over, I wasn't ready to leave my cocoon. After months and months of being at home with just my kids, I felt like I was a shadow of my former self. When I got to the point where I was doing everything I could to avoid leaving the house, I knew I had to do something. I tried to continue to use Covid as an excuse…"oh I'm part of the vulnerable sector; I still need to be careful". The truth was that I was afraid to bump into anybody I knew because I was so ashamed of my body. It's easy to hide those extra pounds on a Zoom call. The funny thing is, I wasn't even aware of why I was hiding. I had myself convinced that it was a safety thing and not a body shame thing. Yes, a lot of people had gained weight and let themselves go during lockdown, but because of my past experiences and low self esteem I felt like I was the only one.

Today is about recognizing the way you truly feel about yourself.

- Make a list of at least five things you like about yourself:

- I AM:
- I AM:
- I AM:
- I AM:
- I AM:

- Now make a list of five things that you dislike about yourself:

- Which list was more difficult to write out? Why? What does this tell you about how you feel about yourself right in this moment?

day 2: the feel wheel

TODAY'S AFFIRMATION: *My body deserves to be loved.*

- The 'Feel Wheel' diagram on the next page has 12 sections. Each section represents either a positive or negative feeling or viewpoint that you may have about yourself
- Starting in the center of the wheel, color each section so that it represents how often or how strongly you have these feelings on a scale of 1-10. (Each of the rings represents a number from 1-10.)
- Use any color(s) you like for the positive feelings, and use black for the negative feelings.
- What does your 'Feel Wheel' look like? How colorful is it? How lopsided is it? Do you think this misshapen wheel might prevent you from traveling forward? How does this make you feel?

Sandy Lynn

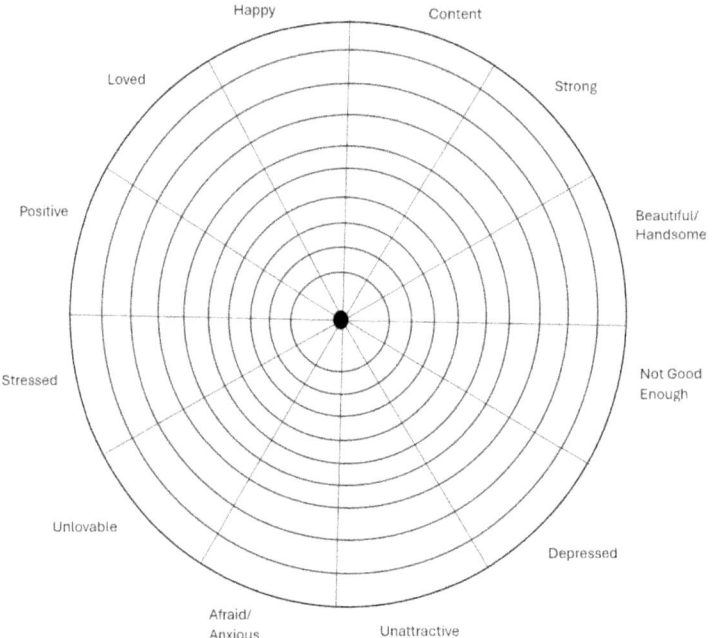

day 3: going down the right rabbit hole

TODAY'S AFFIRMATION: *Everything about me is beautiful, regardless of anyone else's opinion.*

I OFTEN HEAR people use the term 'rabbit hole', especially in reference to social media. Like, "OMG I just went down the TikTok rabbit hole and before I knew it two hours had gone by." Losing time is not the only problem with social media rabbit holes. The biggest question here is: why do we need these distractions? Most of the time it's because we are avoiding something. More often than not we are trying to avoid going down our own personal rabbit hole. The one in which we have to dive down and face what we are truly feeling about ourselves, and why we feel that way. There's a common saying: You have to feel it to heal it. But, in order to feel it, you have to actually acknowledge it and face it. So today we are going to explore your own rabbit hole.

Answer the following questions as honestly as you can. Don't think about it too much, just answer with whatever immediately comes to your mind:

- Do you love yourself?

- Are you important?

- What is the best thing about you?

- What is your most attractive body part?

- How do you handle it when you make a mistake?

- How do you feel/react when someone criticizes you?

- What are you really good at?

- When you're laying in bed getting ready to go to sleep, do you think about what you did well that day, or what you did wrong?

- If you could do anything with your life, what would it be?

When you're finished read through your answers again. Did anything surprise you? What have you learned about yourself? What can you work on that might help change your beliefs and be less critical of yourself?

day 4: think about who you're talking to

TODAY'S AFFIRMATION: *I am kind to others. I deserve and offer that same kindness to myself.*

IT IS SO important that we are aware of how we talk to and about ourselves, both privately and in public. This hit me quite hard when one of my friends pointed out that I had just referred to myself as an 'old, fat broad'. Even though I was trying to be funny, I was still referring to myself in a negative manner. Learn to realize when you are using self-deprecating language, even if it does come out camouflaged as humor.

Imagine that you're just hanging out with one of your close friends and he/she said, "I'm so fat", "I'm so ugly", "No one would ever want to date me," or any kind of similar statement.

- What would you say to him/her?

- Now, read what you just wrote to your friend and repeat it to yourself out loud.

day 5: mirror, mirror

TODAY'S AFFIRMATION: *My body is a beautiful gift and I feel blessed to have received it.*

UNDRESS DOWN TO YOUR UNDERWEAR, or more if you feel comfortable doing so. Now stand in front of the mirror and spend at least five minutes looking at yourself. See your entire body from head to toe. Make a mental note of how you feel about everything you see, what you like and dislike.

Light your favorite candle. Write down everything you disliked on a piece of paper. Include any negative feelings you felt, any criticisms that came to mind, and any negative statements you said to yourself, whether outloud or in your head.

Then fold this piece of paper in half, facing away from you. Fold it once or twice more, always facing away from you. Now burn it and blow the ashes away (or rinse them down the sink with water). You can also tear it into tiny pieces and let it go in the trash. While you are 'getting rid of' these negative statements, say Today's Affirmation out loud as many times as you need to.

day 6: self care check in

TODAY'S AFFIRMATION: *I need and deserve to put myself before anyone else.*

WHEN I WAS GROWING up I often felt like an outsider. I would watch my mom and my sister interact with each other, playing little games and singing silly songs; and I felt like I was on the outside looking in. There were a lot of reasons for this (that would be another book all on its own) but I think now that a lot of it had to do with my mom's feelings of guilt. She got pregnant at a young age and had to get married. I truly believe that her fear, guilt and shame was passed on to me while I was still in the womb. When my sister came along, Mom was already a married woman and it was her second pregnancy so she was able to enjoy it a bit more. I also dealt with issues of abandonment because of my dad leaving the family. My self esteem and feelings of self worth were almost non-existent. I was never able to say no if I was asked for something or asked to do something. I became the person that everyone counted on, the "people pleaser'.

As I grew into an adult these feelings of inadequacy continued to haunt me and to control my life. I ended up getting quite ill, physically and mentally. I was depressed, and I was moving through life just numb. I was existing, not living. This is when I realized that I needed to start taking care of myself. It was so difficult because the feelings of guilt and selfishness were hard to battle. But I realized this: When I'm putting myself first and doing what I need to do, I feel happier. I have more to give the people around me. I am overall a better and stronger healer. My family and my kids are more balanced – even now that they're adults. I have more to give them, because I keep my own cup full.

Today you will have a quick check-in with yourself and look at how well you practice self-care. Answer the following questions honestly:

- How am I feeling today?

- Why am I feeling this way?

- How do I want to feel when I wake up in the morning?

- What was I doing the last time I felt truly happy?

- Am I getting enough sleep?

- Am I getting enough exercise?

- Am I taking time to relax?

- When I give advice to others, do I follow it myself?

- When did I last enjoy quiet time to myself?

- What are hobbies/activities that I enjoy doing for myself?

- When was the last time I did any of these activities?

- Are there any new things I want to try?

- What are my goals for the next week/month/year?

- If I knew there was absolutely no way I could fail, and other people's opinions didn't matter, what would I most like to do with my life?

day 7: free write

TODAY'S AFFIRMATION: *I am clearing away the negativity of my past and I am making space for my exciting future!*

TODAY IS A 'FREE WRITE'. Write about any feelings you had while completing this week's exercises. Were there any surprises? What did you learn about yourself? How did you do with this week's Challenge? Feel free to write about anything and everything that comes into your head. Get it out, free your mind, put it on the paper.

Sandy Lynn

Complete this statement: I AM

step 2: unlearning the past

"Life can only be understood backward, but it must be lived forward."
Soren Kierkegaard

THE JOURNEY to healing is an interesting one. I started on my path a few years ago, and as I make my way through this process I often find myself thinking about everything that has brought me to this point. I was stuck for a long time. Stuck in some kind of limbo between living and existing. I was trying to live, but the barriers of my past kept me from reaching my full potential. I was going through my days in a fog, feigning enthusiasm for things that no longer interested me, investing everything in my children and their activities. I would tell myself that I was a parent now and my main focus was to give my children everything they needed. And I will never regret that because they were my only source of joy for a very long time. And by focusing on what they needed, I didn't have to pay any attention to what I needed. I was making my way numbingly through each and every day…go to work, feed the family, take the kids to baseball, evening chores, watch TV and go to bed…day after day after day.

When I look back on that time with the 'healed perspective' that I have now, I realize that the numbness I was feeling had a lot to do with the fact that I had spent my entire life in fight or flight mode. I do not remember a time when I ever truly felt safe. No wonder I wasn't feeling anything. I was trapped in what you might call a 'pain loop'; not healing, but not knowing how to move forward. And the pain that I was feeling was the pain of my Inner Child. She had been through so much, but I had never acknowledged her grief. I needed to reach that point where I could stop and realize that almost everything I had been told or learned about myself during my childhood was a lie. I had no idea that it's ok to have feelings, it's ok to talk about problems and it's ok to ask for help. I was taught pretty much the opposite of this, so I had a lot of learning to do. I had to review what I had learned about relationships. I had to learn that it's ok to be a strong woman; that I didn't have to be submissive to my male counterpart. I had to learn that sex is not a bad thing. I wouldn't be able to feel the grief of my Inner Child until I was able to recognize that a lot of the things that she had experienced did not have to be accepted as 'just a part of life.'

So how did I do that? Well…the first thing I learned was that learning new lessons is NOT the difficult part; it's UNlearning the old lessons that kicks you in the ass. I had to be willing to go deep. I had to be willing to open up and recognize that the things that I had experienced were not necessarily 'normal' or acceptable. I had to admit to myself that maybe the significant people in my life were not always right and didn't always do the right things for me. That was hard because these were people I loved and respected. But I had to remind myself that realizing that they made mistakes is not disrespecting them, but giving me the chance to finally respect myself.

I also had to learn to feel. I had to feel the pain of my Inner Child. I had to cry every tear she never shed. I had to speak every word she wanted to say but didn't. I had to feel the anger, and the fear and the loneliness that she buried because she deserved the chance to feel all of it and know that it was real. Just recently I spent almost an entire Breathwork session sobbing because I felt such profound sadness for this little girl. I had to show her the compassion that she had never been shown so that I could let her go. It's almost like I had to see that damaged Inner Child as a separate person and allow her to pass on to a better place. She's been through enough. I mourned her loss as if I were mourning for my closest friend. But at the same time, I felt such a huge sense of relief as I knew it was finally time for her to rest.

The great thing about healing is that you realize that your Inner Child is like a Phoenix. This means that you have the ability to rise from the flames and be reborn as a stronger, fiercer version of your previous self. This version is filled with hope. There is a better, more joyful way to live life and they want it. They wear the pain and lessons of their previous self like badges of honor because these are the gifts that have made you the amazing person that you are today. This version is grateful for each and every step that has been taken on this journey, and the further down the path of life that you travel the more your vision of a brighter future expands. Are you ready to become who you were always meant to be?

week 2: where do my beliefs about myself come from?

"Intelligence is what we learn. Wisdom is what we unlearn."
JR Rim

NOW THAT YOU'VE recognized how you feel about yourself, it's time to take an honest look at your thought patterns. Your thoughts shape your world. The interesting thing is that most of your thoughts are not your own. They're connected to the people, experiences, and messages that you receive from your environment while you're growing up. I teach sociology at the local college, and one of the basic concepts that I teach my students is the process of *socialization.* Socialization is the concept that your thoughts and ideas and beliefs are basically created for you by your surroundings. For most people the major agent of socialization is their family unit, because that's their first exposure to the world around them. Essentially everything that you learn about your place in the world comes from those people who are immediately surrounding you. This means that many of your beliefs are created for you before you're even born. They are then solidified in your personality in childhood through your experiences, then reinforced for the rest of your life. These can be as automatic as your language, the food you eat, or your religious beliefs. They can be as simple as how you tie your shoelaces, and as complex as the way you view yourself in this world.

In my case, I grew up with a lot of feelings of inadequacy. I never felt like I was good enough and because of that, I *believed* that there was something wrong with me. There are many reasons, situations and events that helped me to form that belief. These issues stuck with me for most of my life. I never thought to question these beliefs. To me, it was just the way things were. It was the way I had always known them to be. Some people were destined to be pretty and successful and happy; others were not. Your lot in life just depended on the 'luck of the draw' and there was nothing you could do about it. I was basically taught that having dreams was a waste of time because your life was going to be what it was going to be and there was nothing that you could do about it. The best thing that I could hope for was to finish school and get a half decent job, find a good man to marry and raise a nice little family. The funny thing is that I had a feeling all along, ever since I was a young child, that there was something special about me. There was something that I was meant to do that would make a difference. I just had no idea what it was, and to be honest these thoughts were soon squashed by my mother who wanted me to just face reality so that I wouldn't be disappointed. I don't blame her for that, it was all she knew. And it then became all that I knew.

In fact, for my family, it was like if you did expand your horizons or become more than was expected of you, you should brush it under the rug. I really felt it when I went back to school and completed my Masters Degree. Sometimes I was almost made to feel embarrassed by it. It would be put forward like you were being teased: "Oh so you're so much better than the rest of us now, ha ha ha." But when I think back about it, it was almost resentment coming through because I had dared to try and break the cycle. Or when someone in the family spent money on some kind of extravagance that was deemed frivolous or unnecessary there were a lot of hushed conversations about how they didn't really need that car or that trip and how foolish it was of them to have spent the money on it. It took me a long time to learn that I didn't have to continue to carry on these beliefs and I didn't have to hide my dreams. As your life changes, as your experiences change, so can your beliefs. It was very hard to get used to but it's actually very liberating to realize that you can 'dump' these negative thoughts and beliefs that you have been carrying (and that didn't even belong to me) and have my own.

The thing is, as long as your negative beliefs about yourself and your world go unnoticed and unchallenged, you are not living intentionally. Your life is on autopilot and instead of being proactive, you're being reactive. This is why you keep making the same mistakes, experiencing the same pain and feeling the same disappointments over and over again. You need to learn what your core beliefs are, because not knowing is the driving force behind your self sabotage. That will help you learn your triggers. Then you can set goals to change your behavior. No one deserves to live in pain. You deserve happiness. It's time to break these cycles of negativity and take charge of your life in a powerful and positive way.

This week, we will be looking at your internalized beliefs about yourself and your place in the world. We'll be challenging them, so that in coming weeks we can replace them with beliefs that actually serve you and your vision of your future.

Weekly Challenge: For this entire week every time you see your reflection, whether it's in a mirror, a window, or a puddle, smile and say something kind to yourself. If you can't think of something kind, say, "I love you."

This Week's Meditation: Week 2–Recognizing Self Limiting Beliefs

day 1: getting to know your inner bully

TODAY'S AFFIRMATION: *Every moment is a new beginning. This is mine.*

MANY OF US have watched the movie 'Mean Girls'. Maybe you've been bullied or witnessed someone being bullied. I remember watching the movie and thinking, "How can people treat another human being like that?" But have you ever paid attention to the way you talk to yourself? I know that I have looked in the mirror and told myself that I'm disgusting, gross, fat. I never once stopped to think, "How can I treat myself like that?" This is your Inner Bully.

On a sheet of paper, write a letter to yourself from your Inner Bully. What does he/she say to you on a regular basis? Hear the voice in your head. Don't hold back! If your Bully is being mean, be mean. Get it all out on the paper.

When you are done, read it out loud to yourself. Let yourself feel all of the feelings when you hear yourself say the words. Cry if you need to, yell if you need to.

When you are finished, light a candle, Then fold the piece of paper in half, facing away from you. Fold it once or twice more, always facing away from you. Now burn it and blow the ashes away (or rinse them down the sink with water). You can also tear it into tiny pieces and let it go in the trash. While you are letting go of your Bully's words, say TODAY'S AFFIRMATION out loud as many times as you need to.

day 2: who's got the power?

TODAY'S AFFIRMATION: *The most important voice in my life is my own.*

I HAVE MENTIONED before the idea of 'you have to feel it to heal it'. I know that it's hard. When I first began this journey and started to allow myself to feel things after bottling up my emotions for so many years I thought the tears would never stop. I came to so many realizations that had never occurred to me. I discovered that I wasn't being strong, I was hiding. By not feeling anything I could avoid the pain, but I was living in a state of numbness. I cannot tell you what a weight has been lifted and how much my life has changed. So yes, it's hard…but it is so worth it!

How did you feel when you read the letter from your Inner Bully yesterday?

Now think about where this Bully got his/her power. Be honest with yourself. This is where that inner negative voice comes from. Write about this. Use the following prompts or just write whatever comes to your mind.

- Did you hear the voice of anyone in particular? It could even be more than one person, or maybe you aren't exactly sure where your Bully's power comes from.

- Did any specific events from your childhood come to mind?

When you feel like you are finished, read what you wrote. Reassure yourself that the voice you heard is not your own.

day 3: pay no attention to the man behind the curtain

TODAY'S AFFIRMATION: *I live my life in the present moment.*

LET'S continue taking apart this Inner Bully of yours. Continue to just write from the heart whatever comes to mind. Think again about all of the things your Bully said to you in the letter.

- Think about who's voice(s) might be talking to you through this bully.
- Were these your truths? Or theirs? Remember that hurt people hurt people. Most likely they were projecting their pain onto you and not even realizing it.
- But is it your responsibility to carry their pain?

Sandy Lynn

When you are done writing, read it. Does anything surprise you? Are you ready to let it all go?

day 4: it's not fair to compare

TODAY'S AFFIRMATION: *I have no room in my heart or mind for insecurity.*

AS A CHILD I used to daydream constantly about what my life would be like under different circumstances. I would climb up into the big willow tree in our front yard. About half way up there was the perfect branch for sitting on. I would sit there for hours and read and dream. I would dream that my dad came home and professed his undying love for my mom, my sister and I, promising never to leave us again. I would dream that I was adopted and my real parents were coming back to take me away with them to a beautiful home where I was so loved and I took singing lessons and dancing lessons. I would think about my friends and their families and wish I could live with them. When we are unhappy within ourselves, or we come from a place where we've been made to feel 'less than', we tend to compare our lives to other people's.

. . .

Write from the heart:

- Do you often compare yourself to others?

- Do you judge your life and accomplishments based on other people's?

- Do you feel less than, better than or equal to others? Why do you think you feel this way?

Now think about your answers to the above questions.

- Why do you think you do this?

- Are you being fair when you compare?

- Do the people that you compare yourself to have the same background, life experiences and opportunities as you have had?

day 5: quieting the voice

TODAY'S AFFIRMATION: *I will no longer carry burdens.*

SOMETIMES IT'S hard to fight the things we cannot see. The idea of an Inner Child, or an Inner Bully is hard to comprehend because they are not concrete, and because of that it's difficult for us to acknowledge that they even exist. That's why you'll often find that when healers, both holistic and traditional, are doing Inner Child work they will ask the client to bring a photo of themselves as a child. We can do the same thing with your Inner Bully.

- If you could turn your Inner Bully into a character, what kind of character would it be?

- Is your Bully male or female? Does he/she have a name?

- Older or younger?

- Describe the physical appearance. Describe the voice. Where does he/she live? What is he/she good or bad at?

- When you are done with your character answer the following: Does having an actual person/character help to quiet your inner voice? Does it make it easier to understand that this Inner Bully is not you?

day 6: break up day!

TODAY'S AFFIRMATION: *I accept myself, I love myself and I am moving forward.*

WRITE A 'DEAR JOHN' letter to your Inner Bully. It's time to end the relationship. Let all of your feelings out in this letter. Allow yourself to be sad or angry or whatever you need to be. Let them know why you need to end this relationship.

End the letter on a positive note. Let them know that you understand and appreciate why they did what they did, but that you need to move ahead on your own. Tell them that it's time to step back and let you take the lead.

day 7: free write

TODAY'S AFFIRMATION: *I choose to let go of the past, knowing that I am safe and protected.*

TODAY IS A 'FREE WRITE'. Write about any feelings you had while completing this week's exercises. Were there any surprises? What did you learn about yourself? How did you do with this week's Challenge? Feel free to write about anything and everything that comes into your head. Get it out, free your mind, put it on the paper.

Sandy Lynn

Complete this statement: I AM

week 3: acknowledging self-limiting beliefs

"It's not what you are that holds you back, it's what you think you are not."
Denis Waitley

THIS WEEK we will focus on separating emotions, thoughts, and beliefs. Emotions are chemical reactions in the body. They are triggered by your thoughts and experiences, and they also bring about thoughts that feel similar to the emotion. Most people have trouble expressing how they *feel* about something. When asked what they're feeling during a triggered state, they will almost always respond with a thought: "I feel like I'll never find love." When you remove "I feel like" from this sentence, you're left with a thought: "I'll never find love." Thoughts are filters through which we experience our specific world and the vehicle with which we create our specific reality. Thoughts are things. The problem starts, for many of us, when we allow that thought to become a belief. *A belief is a thought that you've agreed is correct.* Once you've made that agreement it becomes a reality of life for you, and you'll then keep reaffirming that belief through your experiences for as long as the belief is active. As long as the agreement exists, that belief runs as automatic programming underneath everything that you do. It informs every single thing that you do and think.

I spoke in the introduction of this book about how the events of my childhood led to my carrying the belief that I should be ashamed of my body. This week I would like to share a story that might be all too familiar to many of you.My dad left my mom, my sister and I when I was about seven years old. I rarely saw him when I was growing up. Every once in a while my mom would say that he had called and that he was coming to see us. Sometimes he would even show up. Most of the time though, he never showed. I remember sitting on the steps all day…waiting. I would ask my mom over and over, "When's dad coming?" She would sigh and say, "I don't know Sandy." So I'd sit….and sit….convinced that this time he would finally show up. My younger sister Terry would give up and go play, but I refused to move. Every time I heard a vehicle coming up the road my heart would beat faster. I'd jump up trying to get a glimpse of his car; but it was never his car. I would start making up excuses for him in my mind: he had to work late, his car broke down, he was sick. I never asked myself why he didn't call and I never gave up hope. Every time he told mom he was coming, I was sure he was coming. Finally, once it started to get dark, mom would come out and tell me in a soft voice, "It's time to come in now Sandy. It's late and you need to get ready for bed. I don't think he's coming anymore today." Then she'd hug me and keep her arm draped around me as we went inside. At some point she just stopped telling us that he had called and if he did show up, which was rare, it was a surprise for us.

Experiencing this over and over again from a young age left a firmly engraved message in my young mind. I wasn't worth it. I wasn't worth his time. I wasn't even worth a phone call to say he wouldn't be coming. I felt very unloved. Removing the feeling made this a thought: "I am unloved." I then made an agreement with this thought and allowed it to become a belief: "I am unlovable; I am not enough." I carried this belief into my adult relationships and because of it I allowed myself to be mistreated. I had no idea what boundaries were. I believed that I was the problem so I just kept trying and trying to be better; to be worthy of love. Any time I was mistreated or abused there was a part of me that believed that I deserved it. I did not have the tools to break the agreement, and then change the belief. Even receiving compliments was difficult for me. I constantly deflected or came up with a reason that I didn't deserve the compliment. Recently someone told me: "There are two ways to respond to someone who gives you a compliment: a 'thank you' or a' fuck you'. The thing is, anything that is not a 'thank you' is a 'fuck you'." That was a real eye opener for me.

There are numerous studies that delve into the effect of childhood experiences on adult behavior. It is well known that the early years are the most crucial and can affect all areas of development from social/emotional to behavior to language. And if we look at some of the more popular treatments that therapists are using today, we can see the correlation between our thoughts, feelings and beliefs and how they affect each other. Cognitive Behavioural Theory (CBT) for example, focuses on the fact that our thoughts, feelings, behaviors, and even body sensations are all connected. The way we respond to an event will be rooted in how we interpret or perceive that event. For example, if I text a friend and my friend doesn't respond I can perceive this in different ways. I might think, "Oh wow she must be really angry with me about something. What have I done?" This might leave me feeling anxious and unsettled. Or I might think, "That's so unlike her. She must be having a really busy day. I hope everything is ok." This leaves me feeling concerned for my friend. The way I react depends on how I perceive the situation, and the way I perceive the situation depends on my own positive or negative life experiences. This explains why two different people might react differently to the same situation. They are perceiving it differently based on their own beliefs and life experiences. If this is the case, then what we think and do, will affect the way that we feel. In fact, in his article *Health and Happiness Go Hand In Hand* published by Harvard Health in 2021, Matthew Solan talks about the 50-40-10 rule of happiness: "Research suggests that, on average, 50% of people's general level of happiness is determined by genetics. However, 40% is under people's control, and the remaining 10% depends on the circumstances" (Solan, 2021)

What this means then, is that our beliefs can be challenged and changed. You are not your thoughts; you are not your emotions; you are not your beliefs. What you believed at one point in your life might not be the same later in life. The easiest way to think about it is to go back to some of the things that many of us believed in as children. In my culture these were entities such as Santa Claus, The Easter Bunny, or even the Tooth Fairy. At one point in your young lives you believed in one or all of these things, or something similar, with your entire being. As you grew into an adult those beliefs (unfortunately) changed. Our beautiful, positive childhood beliefs were replaced with the 'reality' of adulthood. But the great part about having the ability to change our beliefs also means that we can change and let go of any negative beliefs and replace them with positive ones. YOU have power over your thoughts and, therefore, over your beliefs and emotions. We all go through the process of socialization, where our beliefs and values are given to or projected onto us from the people and the environment that surrounds us. As you mature, however, it's your choice as to whether or not you want to agree with those thoughts and keep believing in them. There are so many people who have broken their agreements with limiting thoughts. Maybe their family is racist and they've broken that agreement and chosen not to be. Or they were born into a certain religion and left that religion because their values and beliefs changed. What you choose to believe is essentially up to you.

Let's look at our beliefs and our emotions and where they come from. I have mentioned before that a lot of my self-limiting beliefs have to do with my body. A lot of this stems from my childhood. At one point I was rarely leaving the house. I had the best intentions; I wanted to do things. Friends would call me up and ask me to go out somewhere or do something and I would jump up and say yes! Most times I was very excited about it and looked forward to it. The day would come and I would do my hair and put on my makeup and think, "yeah, I look good!" And then came the time to get dressed. And that's when the trouble would start. I would put on outfit after outfit until I had clothes thrown all over the room because after putting on each one I would look in the mirror and think, "Nope! I'm so fat! I look disgusting!" I had the thought that I was overweight, and then I made an agreement with that thought that turned into the belief that I looked disgusting. It took me a long time and a lot of work to cancel that agreement. So when you are in a triggered or emotional state, ask yourself, "How do I feel? Is it a belief or an emotion?" An emotion is things like "I feel overwhelmed. Sad. Frustrated." A belief is things like, "I feel like I'm never going to find love." "I feel like this sort of thing always happens to me." "I feel like no one understands me." Remember that when you remove "I feel like" you are left with the limiting belief.

This week we are going to take a long hard look at your

negative thoughts, your self limiting beliefs. What are they? Where do they come from? How do they affect you in your daily life? How can you change them? Again, the key here is to be absolutely honest with yourself. The deeper you can go, the more healing that will take place. Once you become aware of these beliefs you can then look at the thoughts that they come from. The thoughts that YOU made the agreement with; and then you can focus on breaking those agreements and making new ones. Better agreements with more positive thoughts.

Weekly Challenge: This week's challenge is all about awareness. Focus on how you are speaking to yourself. What is your inner voice saying? What is the tone of your inner voice? Is it critical? Is it judgmental? Are you being hard on yourself? Listen for that inner voice, be aware of it, and take notes. Journaling about this will also be very helpful.

This Week's Meditation: Week 3–Developing Positive Self Talk

day 1: recognizing your mindset

TODAY'S AFFIRMATION: *I am perfect just as I am.*

OUR NEGATIVE THOUGHTS can be placed into different categories. Some of us engage in catastrophizing, which means that no matter the situation we are going to expect the worst. This was, and sometimes still is, a big one for me personally: I can't do this because then this will probably happen. Some of us personalize, which means that we take all fault and responsibility upon ourselves. There are those of us who filter our thoughts, choosing to magnify the negative in every situation. To use the old cliche, we see the glass half empty. And finally, there is polarizing. Everything about a situation is either positive or negative; there is no in between. I challenge you to ask yourself: Do any of these sound familiar? Let's look then, at the source of your beliefs.

Journal about the following question without overthinking it. Just write whatever comes to mind:

- What are some of the negative thoughts you have in your mind throughout the day?

- Do you recognize that you think in these ways? Is there a pattern?

- Do you catastrophize, personalize, polarize or filter?

day 2: the peanut gallery

TODAY'S AFFIRMATION: *I choose my standards of success.*

WHEN I WAS GROWING up I heard a lot of comments about weight and body size. My mom often chastised me if she felt my top was too low cut and I was showing too much cleavage; which was hard to get away from sometimes because I did have a very large bust. I was also a teenager back in the '80s when music videos were just starting to come out and heavy metal 'hair' bands had a lot of scantily clad women in their videos. This gave us the impression that sexy women were very skinny with large breasts and tight bodies...nothing should jiggle. It was also the era of skin tight jeans. I remember so many times helping a friend pull up the zipper of her jeans with a coat hanger. And then I also remember having a family member comment on how I was trying to shove 20 pounds of meat in a 10 pound bag. With the body issues that I already had, in my mind he was talking about my fat body not my skin tight jeans.

Today though, it seems that large, jiggly butts are the goal. The jigglier the better. It's so hard to keep up with what the world wants. The media has started to acknowledge and feature plus size models, which is wonderful. But if you really take a look at these models, they still have great big boobs, great big butts, and tiny waists. From a young age, the media bombards us with some ideal image of perfection, and lets us know when we are not living up to that ideal. Not long ago a movie came out titled, "The DUFF", in which a teenage girl discovers she is known as the Designated Ugly Fat Friend in her friend group. This is just one example of how our society reinforces the almost impossible benchmarks that both women and men are striving to live up to. When people try to send any message that does not coincide with these benchmarks, they are criticized. I remember falling in love with Meagan Trainor's song, "All About The Base". Finally, someone has acknowledged that big can be beautiful. But even though she had a wonderful message behind her song, some called the song an example of skinny-shaming.

- What comments did you hear about bodies growing up from family members, friends or the media?

- In some families, there are no compliments, there's only criticism. Was this the case in your family?

day 3: criticism, envy or judgement?

TODAY'S AFFIRMATION: *I have no room for comparison, judgment or insecurity in my life. I choose to focus on my own journey.*

WE OFTEN JUDGE or feel envious of others. This is actually a form of self rejection or a distraction from what we're judging and rejecting in ourselves. If we're judging someone else, the logic is that we're not coming down so hard on ourselves. But actually the opposite is true because the self-judgment doesn't actually go away. It only becomes masked, which makes it harder to release. My friend Ellie said that she remembers a time when she would look at people with very athletic bodies, who clearly worked out a LOT, and judge them as shallow. "There's an idiot." "That person is insecure." Then one day she started dating one of *those* people and now she works out six days a week and is a gym addict herself! The shift happened when she realized that taking care of the body is actually a part of the spiritual work. "How can you work toward being your most evolved self if you're rejecting the body?"

I remember walking into my first burlesque dance class and looking at what the women were wearing. Inside my head one voice was saying, "Wow, it's so great that you have no body issues and are comfortable wearing that outfit". But, the other voice inside my head was arguing: "She is the same size as me and I would not be caught dead in that outfit because I would look ridiculous". When you think about the way you're judging other people, you're judging yourself the same way. I realized that I was judging others because I saw a deficiency in myself. Like the mean girls – picking on and making fun of a girl because her skirt's too short or her top shows too much, but actually they kind of wish they looked like her and that they were getting the attention that she was getting.

- When you look at the body types around you, what are your judgments? This is your inner dialogue that you would never say out loud to anyone. Be VERY honest about this.

day 4: i believe

TODAY'S AFFIRMATION: *My past experiences do not hold me back.*

WE ALL HAVE specific beliefs about our bodies. Some of mine for example would be: My belly is too big. My arms are too flabby. My shoulders are too broad. No one's going to love me unless I lose 20 pounds. I remember when I was younger one of my older family members told me that I shouldn't worry about losing weight because if you meet a man when you're a little overweight you know that he loves you for you. In her opinion it was normal for women to gain weight after having children or as they age, and that does not go over well with men who married skinny women. In her eyes, it was better to meet a man when you're fat! But the thing is, it's not the weight or the shape of your body that keeps you from everything you want. It's your mindset. There are so many people who are so successful and do not have perfect bodies. They are dealing with a lot of the same things that you are judging and being hard on yourself for. The difference is the way that they view themselves. The way that they love themselves just the way they are. You don't have to change anything about yourself in order to have what you want. You have to accept yourself for who you are. It's our differences and the variety that makes us unique and interesting.

- What beliefs do you hold about yourself? Make a list of all the thoughts and beliefs you have about your body. Be specific and be brutally honest. Some of these beliefs could be: I am not attractive, I'm not the 'pretty one', I need to lose/gain weight to find love.

- How does the way that you were raised affect your beliefs about yourself today?

- What self-limiting beliefs do you have that stem from your childhood?

day 5: thoughts and beliefs

TODAY'S AFFIRMATION: *All I need is my own approval.*

IN THE INTRODUCTION to this week I made the statement: *A belief is a thought you've agreed is correct.* And once you've made that agreement, you keep reaffirming it until it becomes an actual belief. As long as this belief exists, it will affect everything you think, say and do. Yesterday you wrote about the self-limiting or negative beliefs that you have about yourself. Essentially what you've done is you've made a contract with these beliefs. In order to change your thinking you must be willing to break these contracts. Take a look back at what you wrote yesterday.

- What are the agreements you've made?

- The false beliefs you've fostered?

- Are you prepared to break the contract you've formed with these beliefs?

Next week we will talk more about how to prepare yourself to break the contracts and create new positive ones. For now, I would like you to give your beliefs a name. For example, I've decided to name my belief that I am too fat, Bob. Once you have named your self-limiting beliefs, write down some different strategies for how you can begin to change the hold they have over you. Are you going to protect Bob, ignore Bob, sit down and observe Bob, learn more about Bob and where he comes from? All of these strategies will be preparing you to say goodbye to Bob, break the contract, and develop a new, positive belief about yourself.

day 6: releasing

TODAY'S AFFIRMATION: *I am allowed to create a life I want to live.*

TODAY I WANT you to think about what kind of future is possible for you if you release these self limiting beliefs? Anything you want becomes possible when you can see it with clarity. If you want to love yourself more, you have to imagine what that might look and feel like.

Journal about what you see when you ask yourself these questions:

- How might my life change?

- How do my interactions with others change?

- How do I show up in your life and in my relationships?

- How do I feel when I set boundaries or communicate my needs?

- How do people treat me differently when I set boundaries and communicate my needs?

day 7: free write

TODAY'S AFFIRMATION: *I am proud of how far I've come.*

TODAY IS A 'FREE WRITE'. Write about any feelings you had while completing this week's exercises. Were there any surprises? What did you learn about yourself? How did you do with this week's Challenge? Feel free to write about anything and everything that comes into your head. Get it out, free your mind, put it on the paper.

Sandy Lynn

Complete this statement: I AM

week 4: changing thought patterns

"We have the power to choose who and how we want to be in the world, each and every moment, regardless of what external circumstances we find ourselves in."
Dr. Jill Bolte Taylor

MANY OF US suppress our emotions. This is something that we learn in childhood, and it is often a difficult habit to break. I come from a family that was very stoic. Emotions like sadness, anger and frustration are considered useless. After all, once something was done, it was done and you couldn't change it. No sense crying over spilled milk. On top of that, my feelings of self worth were pretty much non-existent. Instead of allowing my emotions to release I became the glue that held everything together, and to be honest, it felt good when people recognized me for it. The only problem is, it was very unhealthy for me. Shutting down an emotion doesn't resolve it, it strengthens it, because you're not letting it pass through and be processed. And sometimes, these emotions become so strong that they begin to have a life of their own.

When I was in my mid 30's I went through a very stressful six month period. My mother was diagnosed with breast cancer, my husband was going through some very serious mental health issues, and my grandmother passed away. She was my best friend. Through it all, I never shed a tear, I never broke down, and I never let anyone know what I was going through. I had two young children to look after and protect. A lot of my closest friends did not know what I was dealing with. A couple of years later my husband and I went to see one of my favorite comedians, Martin Short. This was a comedian that I used to watch a lot as a young teenager. As I watched the show and he went through all of his characters I noticed that I was beginning to feel very emotional. We barely made it back to the car before the tears came, and by the time we got home I was crying uncontrollably. Everything had finally caught up with me; and something about the show had hit a trigger button. The dam broke and I cried all night long and well into the next day. My poor husband had no idea what to do because he wasn't used to seeing me cry. Unfortunately I learned nothing from this, and no one was any the wiser. The only person who had witnessed my emotional breakdown was my husband, so when I was finished crying I shut my emotions down again for another five or six years.

Dr. Jill Bolte Taylor talks about the '90 Second Rule' when it comes to emotions. The rule is that when an event happens, the stress hormones will flood your body for up to 90 seconds and then they're gone. 90 seconds. That's all it takes for stress to come and go. So why then, do our feelings stay with us for so long? I've already talked about how thoughts and emotions are connected, and they are both connected to brain chemistry as well. For most of us, we keep replaying events in our mind, which stimulates our emotions, which then causes the brain to keep pumping adrenaline through our bodies. This means that we can actually *choose* to stop the emotional reactions and, therefore, stop the stress. When you are having an emotional reaction just pause, take a breath and let it happen. Set a timer for 90 seconds or take note of the time on your phone. Notice where you feel it in your body. Give it a name (anger, sadness, fear etc.). Then let it pass through you. Let it go.

Last week I talked about how emotions are chemical reactions in the body that are triggered by your thoughts and experiences. If you are not releasing these thoughts, you will be unable to process the emotions; so they take up residency in your subconscious. When that happens, you are making the agreement to accept the thoughts as true, and they become beliefs. So, if you learn to allow yourself to acknowledge and experience these emotions, you can then release them before they have a chance to turn into a belief. You can do the same with the self-limiting beliefs that you already have; *if* you are willing to do what you need to in order to break the agreement. You need to allow yourself to process the emotion; you need to feel it to heal it.

Weekly Challenge: Embrace gratitude daily–Start thinking about what you are grateful for and make a list. The challenge is to have a list of 50 things you appreciate about your life by the end of the week.

This Week's Meditation: Week 4–Positive Thought Patterns

day 1: recognizing negativity

TODAY'S AFFIRMATION: *Every time I take a breath I release toxic thinking.*

LET'S start digging a little bit deeper into your negative beliefs. All of our beliefs stem from somewhere; we don't just come up with them on our own. The seeds for many of them are planted during childhood, based on the experiences that we have. I've mentioned previously that my mom and dad married very young because my mom was pregnant with me. My dad was the James Dean type, a rock and roll rebel, drummer in a band. He was a good guy and everyone liked him, but he wasn't really a 'family man' and he definitely wasn't the most faithful husband. I developed a lot of my dad's personality and character traits, especially his love for music. I loved to sing and I was pretty good at it. I sang all the time. It was like therapy for me. Anytime anyone asked me what I wanted to do, I'd say, "I'm going to be a singer." My mom, though, discouraged me from this. She'd say, "Yes, you're good. But there are a lot of good singers out there, and you're never going to make a living at it. So, you might as well let that go." I think this was a big part of my developing the belief that "I'm good, but I'm not good enough." That I'm nothing special. Yeah, I can sing, but I'm nothing special, so why even try to pursue it?

When I think back now, part of my mom's reasons for discouraging me might have been because my dad was in a band, and he was unreliable and irresponsible. Maybe she was trying to keep me away from that. Maybe she was trying to protect me from the heartache of being rejected. We project our own limiting beliefs onto other people. We do this automatically, especially with the people we love. So, our limiting beliefs don't just impact us. They're like weeds. Everywhere we go, we're spreading their seeds. We often do this under the guise of protection. My mom was trying to protect me from disappointment.

For today's journal entry, specifically identify your beliefs:

- What do I believe to be true about myself?

- What are my beliefs concerning my ability to succeed?

- What are my beliefs concerning my ability to make money?

- What are my beliefs concerning my relationships?

- What are my beliefs about my body?

- How do my limiting beliefs impact the lives of those I love?

day 2: what if?

TODAY'S AFFIRMATION: *I release any fear of mistakes and imperfection.*

I NOTICED a lot of changes in my mom after she was diagnosed with cancer. She started to pursue a lot of things that she wanted to do. She went back to college. She joined a women's chorus and sang in a few concerts with them. She continued with this outlook even while battling cancer. Perhaps being faced with her own mortality showed her that you have to go for it while you're here. I found it so interesting when she started singing. Maybe, my mom also always wanted to sing, but never gave herself permission because she didn't think she was good enough – a limiting belief that she projected onto me. The problem with a limiting belief is that it's like a boulder you've attached to yourself; a huge ball and chain. You can't go anywhere while you're choosing to carry it around with you. But you don't have to be faced with your own death to change some of your beliefs and start living the way you really want to live.

You just have to choose to break the chain and leave the ball behind.

- How did your darkest moments shape you into who you are today?

- What do you want that your current beliefs are getting in the way of?

- Look at your current list of limiting beliefs and answer the question: if I didn't have this belief, what could I do in my life?

day 3: empowering yourself

TODAY'S AFFIRMATION: *There are great opportunities waiting for me in this life.*

A FEW YEARS ago I was faced with a huge decision that I struggled with for a long time. I was well into my healing journey and was discovering what my true dreams and goals were. I was figuring out what my heart truly wanted, not what I *thought* I wanted (based on my adoption of what others believed I should do). I had found a healing modality that worked for me: Breathwork, and I believed in it so much that I trained to become a Breathwork Healer myself. I was now faced with the decision as to whether or not to accept a full time administrative position with a great salary, or turn that down and focus on the Breathwork and what I thought my true purpose was. I had to ask myself: "Do I believe in myself enough to turn down this steady income and a job I know I'm good at and take that risk?" My whole life I had been taught not to dream, to always take the sensible route. My instinct was to not take chances, to take the job with the guaranteed steady income. It went against every fiber of my being to turn down the full time job and follow my dreams. It was terrifying, but I knew I had to do it. To be honest, it's still scary sometimes, but during those scary moments it's the positive affirmations that bring back my belief in myself.

Every version of you holds different beliefs. There are millions of possible futures for you. Which future you live is determined by the beliefs that you form within your mind. When you change your beliefs, you literally change your future. Today, we're going to project forward into a life that you actually want to live, and we're going to examine what beliefs that version of you holds. Think back to last week's exercise where you defined your ideal future, and also to yesterday when you identified the life you might have if you're not limited by your beliefs. Find a version of you who is truly thriving and living the life you want. Nothing is out of your reach. Answer the following questions that you answered earlier this week, but this time answer as if you were the healed, empowered version of yourself, living the life that you want to live:

- What does my empowered self believe to be true about myself?

- What are my empowered self's beliefs concerning my ability to succeed?

- What are my empowered self's beliefs concerning my ability to make money?

- What are my empowered self's beliefs concerning my relationships?

- What are my empowered self's beliefs about my body?

- How do my empowered beliefs impact the lives of those that I love?

day 4: reframing your thoughts

TODAY'S AFFIRMATION: *I focus on the positive and draw joy from within.*

NEGATIVE THOUGHTS WILL ALWAYS COME, because we're conditioned societally and by our primitive brain to assess risk all the time. The trouble is that most of our negative thoughts are like instinctive reactions. It's like a form of subconscious protection. But if we allow the negative thoughts to control our decisions they will, in fact, diminish the quality of our lives. It's important to recognize negative thoughts and shift them. What we need to learn is how to recognize the negative thought and assess its purpose so that we can then turn it into a positive. You can almost think of it like a thermometer. The negative thoughts are on the bottom, in the cold. What can you do to bring the temperature (or the positivity) up?

In the introduction to this week I talked about the 90 Second Rule of emotions. You can also use that 90 seconds to reframe a negative thought. We know that thoughts and feelings are connected. So if you are feeling a negative emotion, ask yourself if it's connected to a negative thought. For example, for my entire life I have struggled with any type of criticism. Many things that happened in my childhood had turned me into a "people pleaser", so when I was criticized it brought up emotions like anger, sadness, jealousy (of someone who had maybe done better than me). Those feelings were connected to that negative thought or belief that I wasn't good enough. So if I took the 90 seconds and started with the negative emotions (anger, sadness) and connect it to the negative thought of not being good enough, I can then go through what I like to call the *5 R's of Releasing Negative Thoughts:*

- *Recognize* the negative thought. Where does it come from?

- *Reflect* on it. Breathe, count to five.

- *Rationalize* – is this actually true? Do I have proof that it's true?

- *Reframe* – look at alternate perspectives. Instead of "I never do anything right." use, "I sometimes make a mistake."

- *Replace* it with a positive thought

For today's journal exercise I would like you to try reframing some of your negative thoughts:

- What is your biggest negative belief about yourself?

- How does it make you feel?

- Use the 5 R's to reframe it into a positive belief.

- What is a challenge you currently face? How can you reframe this as an opportunity for growth?

day 5: seeing the positive

TODAY'S AFFIRMATION: *I set myself free from negativity.*

I THINK that one of the hardest lessons to learn is to look for the silver lining, to find the positive in the negative. In every situation you are interpreting your situation, circumstances, events, and even yourself. Two different people in the same exact circumstance will have two very different experiences, because your experience depends on your interpretation. How you see yourself determines how you show up. Someone else in your exact body, with your exact intelligence, and your exact circumstances can show up differently because they interpret themselves differently. A good example of this is that we often think that if we had money, status, and fame, we'd be happy. But think about all of the people who do have all these things who become depressed, turn to drugs, or even take their own life. It all depends on your individual perception of the situation.

Right before I started my healing journey, I crashed…hard. I had just gotten out of an extremely narcissistic relationship and I was putting my life back together. I was working for an organization that I had been dedicated to for 25 years. New management had recently taken over, and could see that I was struggling. I made a mistake, and rather than connect with me to ask what happened, or offer support, I got fired immediately. No warning, no discussion, after 25 years of dedication. I was devastated. I had never been fired from a job, ever. A lot of people suggested that I fight back, but I just didn't have it in me at the time. Interestingly enough though, one of my friends said to me, "Sandy, this is the best thing that could have ever happened to you, because you were never going to quit that job. It wasn't challenging to you anymore. It was just a safe place. You were never going to grow or utilize your talents by staying in that position. The universe has set it up so you have no choice but to move forward." At the time I thought that my whole world was falling apart and I couldn't understand what I had done to deserve all of these terrible things that were happening to me. Now I look back and I realize that the relationship and job troubles were blessings in disguise. They were life lessons that taught me how to set boundaries and value myself.

For today's exercise we are going to work on seeing the positives in what seems to be a negative event. We are going to look for the silver lining:

- Think of something that brought joy and describe the moment.

- What elements contributed to this happiness? How can you replicate them?

- Think of an event in the past that felt terrible at the time, but had a positive impact or outcome in your life. Write about it.

- Now, think about a recent negative experience that you've had and describe it. What are the positive aspects that you could pull out of that situation? Where's the silver lining?

day 6: breaking the agreements

TODAY'S AFFIRMATION: *I give myself permission to be authentically me.*

A BELIEF IS an agreement that you've made. Your experience of the world and of yourself is informed by your beliefs. How you interpret the world depends on your beliefs. If you've made the agreement with yourself that you're a terrible public speaker, then every time you have to stand in front of people and share ideas, you'll experience extreme discomfort. If you've made the agreement that you're a great public speaker, you'll have the opposite experience. In the case of negative beliefs, we want to break our agreements with those thoughts.

In his book, *The 4 Agreements*, Don Miguel Ruiz talks about the fact that from the day we are born we are essentially trained to accept society's rules and that these rules keep us from becoming our authentic selves (Ruiz 1997). He states that, instead, we should focus on four main agreements that will bring peace and happiness to our lives:

- Be Impeccable With Your Word.
- Don't Take Anything Personally.
- Don't Make Assumptions.
- Always Do Your Best.

It seems so simple, yet because of our human design we have trouble believing that things can be so simple.

Today you are going to make an official declaration that breaks your agreement with your negative thoughts, so that they are no longer yours. On the following page you will see a template for this declaration. You can use this one, or make one of your own. Think about your negative beliefs and enter them into this declaration. When you are finished, you will sign the declaration, ending the agreement with those beliefs so that you can release them and make agreements with positive thoughts instead. After you have signed it, it's always fun to tear the page out and burn it and really let those negative thoughts go. Fold the page away from you two times, light a candle, say your affirmations, and burn the declaration. Blow the ashes away into the wind or rinse them down the sink and let everything go for good.

My Contract To Break Agreements With My Negative Thoughts

I, _____, do hereby agree to break any and all agreements with the following negative thoughts that I currently have about my physical, emotional or spiritual being:

_____
_____
_____

When these negative thoughts come to mind, I will:

- Recognize the negative thought. Where does it come from?
- Reflect on it. Breathe, count to 5.
- Rationalize – is this actually true? Do I have proof that it's true?
- Reframe – look at alternate perspectives. Instead of "I never do anything right." use, "I sometimes make a mistake."
- Replace it with the following positive thoughts:

_____
_____
_____

To assist me in fulfilling this agreement I will ask the following close friends/family members to hold me accountable if they hear me voice any negative statements about myself:

Sandy Lynn

Signature: _____
Date: _____

day 7: free write

TODAY'S AFFIRMATION: *My attitude is positive and my outlook is bright.*

TODAY IS A 'FREE WRITE'. Write about any feelings you had while completing this week's exercises. Were there any surprises? What did you learn about yourself? How did you do with this week's Challenge? Feel free to write about anything and everything that comes into your head. Get it out, free your mind, put it on the paper.

Sandy Lynn

Complete this statement: I AM

week 5: releasing and letting go

"You can't control every situation, but you can control how you react to it. Choose positivity."
Unknown

THIS WEEK we will continue to find ways to release and let go of what's no longer serving you. There are so many ways to let go of the past, of negative energy, of childhood trauma. You just have to find the method that works for you. I have tried many different ways: meditation, yoga, body talk, journaling. Every day, we learn about releasing techniques that can be used to release negativity in real time. I use several of these techniques on a regular basis and they are all helpful, but the method that helps me the most is Breathwork, which I will talk about more in depth later in this book. Maybe you haven't found exactly what works for you yet and that's okay too; just don't stop trying new things. It took me many years to discover and build my own personal 'program'. I will introduce you to some modalities that I find helpful in a later chapter. The important thing right now is that you continue to take steps, no matter how small they might feel to you.

Healing is a journey. Sometimes it seems like you spend more time broken down on the side of the road, but every mile you travel is worth it. I still have days where I get frustrated and just want to stay wherever it is that I have broken down, pitch a tent and live out the rest of my days. And then I look back to see how far I've come; and I remember what kind of a person I was before I started this journey. I've already talked about my inner shame. Along with that, I was your typical 'yes' woman who put my own needs aside in order to make sure everyone else was happy. Why? Because I was afraid. I didn't have any sense of self-worth, and so I was afraid that people would leave me if I didn't please them and meet all of their needs. I was afraid of conflict so I allowed myself to be mistreated and abused physically, emotionally and mentally. Boundaries? I had no idea what those were. I was so starved for affection and validation from outside that I didn't pay attention to what I felt inside. I don't want to be that person ever again. I feel much better now that I've left her behind. She can stay there in her tent, I'm moving on down the road to the life I deserve.

If you're reading this book, it probably means that you've made the decision to make those changes for yourself. And if you've come this far I want to tell you that I am so proud of you! I know it's not easy. Give yourself a pat on the back, and prepare yourself to begin releasing the past over this next week. Now, just because I say we are going to begin releasing doesn't mean that by the end of the week you will be free of all trauma and instantly jump into a whole new life. Healing is an ongoing journey. To this point you have looked at where your beliefs have come from, acknowledged that some (or maybe many) of these beliefs are self-limiting, and you have begun to change those negative thought patterns. You've done so much work already. If you are really ready to make some changes, you have to be ready to start the process of leaving the past behind and accepting your beautiful self for who you are.

Self-acceptance is, essentially, giving yourself permission to not be perfect. This is different from self-esteem; although many people use these terms interchangeably. Your self-esteem can go up and down based on how you feel about yourself. For many of us, how we feel about ourselves does not come from within us, rather we base it on what we think other people think about us. It's all so confusing. Low self-esteem can be so hard on your mental health, leading to anxiety and depression. Imagine though, if you just gave yourself permission to not be perfect! If you just accepted yourself for who and what you are, without any judgements. Self-esteem can rise and fall, but self-acceptance is constant and steady. If you can do that, you won't be as concerned about what other people think. In turn, your self-esteem will not suffer and, maybe you won't be so hard on yourself.

A big part of self-acceptance is to let go of any of the negative thoughts about yourself that have been planted in your brain. Seeing your worth, overall, rather than focusing on just the negative. As you release what's not serving you, you become more of who you really are. You're able to focus and communicate with more clarity as to what your needs are. You show up more authentically. As you do this, people, situations, circumstances, and things that were aligned with your old self may no longer be in alignment with the new you. They may start to drop away. Are you prepared to let them go?

Weekly Challenge: Be aware of your thoughts this week. Be present and acknowledge how often you might have a negative thought. Take a moment, breathe through it, try changing it into a positive thought. If you can't change it to a positive (and that's ok) just acknowledge the feeling. Breathe in deeply and as you exhale let the negative emotions and feelings go.

This Week's Meditation: Week 5–Learning to Let Go

day 1: learning what you need to let go of

TODAY'S AFFIRMATION: *I let go of what no longer serves me to make space for my dreams.*

WHEN I THINK BACK over my life, I begin to realize that my healing journey started a lot earlier than I originally thought. At the time I didn't realize that the steps I was taking were going to be so critical in my process. Some of the hardest steps to take were those that led me away from people who had been a constant in my life, or to whom I was strongly linked for one reason or another. Probably one of the most difficult and heart-breaking things I have ever had to do was leave my relationship of 20 years with the father of my children.

He and I were both very unhealed when we met, and we tried so hard to make it work. We had many discussions about how we would never damage our children the way we had been damaged. Our relationship, both before and after marriage had many ups and downs over the years, but eventually it got to the point where we were both just going through the motions. I could see that there were some big issues that we needed to deal with, but my husband, who had been through a very traumatizing childhood, preferred to brush it all away and pretend it was all good. This became so much easier for him when he took a job overseas and was gone for eight weeks at a time. When he initially brought forward the idea of taking the job I asked him not to go, as we had so much to work on in our relationship and it would be so hard on the kids. He said it was something he needed to do and told me that he was going whether I liked it or not. This was the beginning of the end.

He worked that job for a year, and each time he came home he was more and more distant. When he got laid off I thought maybe we could finally start again to fix our relationship; but he was just obsessed with finding a way to go back overseas. He admitted to me that he took the job so that he could escape from whatever was going on in his 'real life'. He told me that he loved me as a person and as the mother of his children, but that he didn't know if he was ever really 'in love' with me. He thought maybe that we had fallen into a relationship of convenience and comfort. It was at this point that I realized that staying together was just going to make both of us miserable. I could not see myself living the rest of my life just waiting for him to come home, because even when he was home there was no real interaction. I was exhausted. The kids were old enough to notice that we were not doing well together and had already commented on their dad's detachment. So, I made the decision to leave. It was the best choice for both of us. I remember him telling me that he was proud of me for being able to make the decision and take the necessary steps. He said he knew it needed to be done but that he never would have been able to do it himself. To this day I still have so much love for that man but we both knew we needed to let each other go. My only regret is that my relationship with my stepdaughter was badly damaged. Hopefully we can mend it one day. Until then I continue to love her as if she was my own. My husband unfortunately passed away a few years ago. It was sudden, unexpected and much too soon, but I know that he would be so glad to see that I am finally doing what I have always wanted to do.

Today you are going to look at the people in your life and decide whether or not they are helping you live to your highest good. Is there anybody that you need to let go of? Or at least let go of the hold that their opinions and comments might have over you?

- When you think about your self-limiting beliefs and where they might have come from, is there any particular person that comes to mind?

- Are you prepared to let go of that individual, removing them from your life (it may not need to be permanently) or changing your relationship with them?

- How can you handle this?

- Are there any other people that bring negative energy into your life?

- Write about it. Then read what you wrote. Let it sink in. Are you prepared to let them go?

day 2: it takes practice

TODAY'S AFFIRMATION: *It is safe for me to let go.*

IN HIS BOOK, "LETTING GO", David Hawkins talks about how our unprocessed emotions are causing wounds or blockages that prevent us from realizing our full potential. He explains the importance of processing these emotions so that we can release them. Much like the '90 Second Rule', and the idea of 'you've got to feel it to heal it', Hawkins' "letting go" technique involves allowing the emotion to come forward and letting it run its course. If one can continuously practice this 'letting go' technique:

"You get closer and closer to the real Self and begin to see that you had been duped by feelings all along. You thought that you were the victim of your feelings. Now you see that they are not the truth about yourself; they are merely created by the ego, that collector of programs which the mind has mistakenly believed are necessary for survival." (Bates, 2019)

The idea is that when the emotion comes forward, feel it without any judgment. Let go of any fear of guilt and don't resist. Ignore any thoughts and focus simply on the emotion itself. According to Hawkins, if we allow the feelings to be processed without any thoughts or judgment, we will soon realize that all of these emotions are merely tools that the mind uses to "protect" us; a survival instinct. The more we can learn to 'let go', the more we can undo the damage done by instantly reverting to survival mode. If we can continue to do this, we can free ourselves from attachments and the need for outside validation.

To break it down with a simple example, we've all had those days when someone (a co-worker, employer, friend, family member) has said something that has really triggered or upset us. Let's take this situation and let it go, step by step.

- Being with a feeling–put your attention on the feeling, not the thoughts, no judgments. Do not think about the person or your relationship or the past.
- Focus on what your body feels. (ie. a heaviness in the pit of your stomach). Notice it, watch it.
- Allow the feeling to be there without resisting it (don't tense up your muscles, don't try to force it away).
- Instead, do the opposite–relax and release…relax your shoulders, relax the area of the body in which you feel the feeling, release your tongue from the roof of your mouth.

Remember that letting go doesn't mean the feeling will just go away right away; it means that you're not resisting it. Stay with the feeling, whether it takes two minutes or two days. You may have to come back to it more than once. The more that you practice this, the easier it will get. The instant that you notice a painful feeling, your attention is on it and you can relax.

Find a quiet space where you won't be disturbed. Take a look at what you wrote about yesterday. Practice the above technique. Just focus on the feeling, and then relax. Do this as often as you can throughout the week. Just practice letting go until it gets easier and easier.

day 3: keep it real

TODAY'S AFFIRMATION: *I have the power to overcome my doubts, worries and fears.*

TOWARDS THE END of 2023 I had this feeling building and building inside of me that 2024 was going to be my year. In fact, I started telling my friends this. In my journal I began referring to 2024 as: The Year of Sandy! I had been stepping into a new era of self love. I had been pretty dedicated to making changes in my life so that I could take better care of my mental, physical and spiritual health. Part of this 'new me' was the attitude that I am going to jump into new challenges head first. I wanted to actually do the things that I've always wanted to do and get back to things that make me happy. Things that I had left behind for one reason or another. In late February of 2024 I saw an advertisement for a dance class. Nothing too crazy right? Only it was a high-heels, booty shaking, burlesque style dance class called Vixens. I was intrigued because it seemed to be just the thing I was looking for. Reading the advertisement inspired me because the purpose of this class was to help women build confidence and self esteem, feel comfortable with their bodies, support each other as women and build each other up. What I really liked was that it stated that all ages and body types were welcome to a Vixens Open House session to check it out. I decided that I was going to go…no time like the present to start working towards the goals that I had set for myself.

I ended up taking the class and it was one of the best decisions I have ever made. It was the push I needed to face, head on, the thing that had been holding me back from loving myself unconditionally: love for my physical body. Meeting these fantastic women, feeling the energy of all of us supporting one another, and dancing with them on that stage in front of a sold out crowd was another step toward self-acceptance. I was letting go of the self limiting belief that I wasn't good enough, or skinny enough, or that my body was something I should be ashamed of. It was such an uplifting experience! And it made me realize that I could do absolutely anything that I wanted to do. The only thing holding me back is me!

Today, before you begin to journal I would like you to imagine that you are at the end of your life and you are given an opportunity to travel back in time and speak to your younger self. Your younger self has many questions: "How is our life? Are we happy? Did we do everything we wanted to do?" Write an answer to your younger self that tells the truth about the way you feel you lived your life. Answer their questions. Did you do all you wanted to do? Do you have any regrets?

day 4: what would you change?

TODAY'S AFFIRMATION: *I have the courage and strength to do what is best for me.*

TO CONTINUE with the story I told yesterday, just taking that first step to release my self-limiting belief about my body has led to so many other things! Not only did I feel fantastic about it, but it was so energizing and made me want to do so much more! I signed up for a second round of dance classes but I now also felt confident enough to sign up for musical theater classes! As I write this it dawns on me that I have let go of the fear of singing that was forced upon me and by the end of the year I am going to be singing publicly. Taking that class strengthened so many of my positive thoughts and beliefs that it was also the beginning of my having the courage to write this book! Releasing negative thoughts and self-limiting beliefs is the most wonderful feeling, and once you make up your mind to start it's like a chain reaction!

Review yesterday's entry. Today we will start with the same scenario, but this time you are given the opportunity to go back to the beginning of your life and start over, with the chance to do everything you always wanted to do. This time you are living as your higher self, without the self limiting beliefs, and you are not afraid to take chances.

- What would you change?

- What messages do you want to bring back to your younger self?

- What do you want to be able to tell them about how you lived your life?

day 5: turning the tables

TODAY'S AFFIRMATION: *I focus on what I can control and let go of what I cannot.*

AS WE TRAVEL DOWN the path towards unconditional love and self-acceptance, we often find that we need to change *the way that we think* about what it is that we want out of life. For example, when I was feeling down and depressed about my weight gain, all I kept thinking was, "I wish I was skinny and sexy again. I'm so fat." Taking the dance class helped me to change the *way* that I thought about my body. Maybe it wasn't perfect according to society's standards, but when I'm dancing and performing *I feel good.* Instead of thinking about the way I **look** on the outside, I'm thinking about the way I **feel** on the inside. The more positive and confident I feel, the better I look. The more I dance or workout or do any other kind of exercise, the more my body gets closer to my physical goals. I can't control what other people think of me, so I control what I think of me. Instead of thinking about things from the outside, start thinking about them on the inside. Instead of "I'm sick of being alone, why do I always meet the wrong people?", try "I love myself so I don't mind being alone until I meet someone who loves me the way I love myself". When you start to believe that, and live according to those positive statements, everything else will fall into place.

Today's exercise is to take a good look at the way you think about certain areas of your life and then write your beliefs down in a more positive way.

- About your body
- About your finances
- About your love life
- About your future
- About your relationships

day 6: ready to make new agreements

TODAY'S AFFIRMATION: *Every ending offers me the opportunity for a beautiful new beginning.*

LAST WEEK you made a declaration that broke your agreement with your negative beliefs. This week you are going to make a new agreement…with your positive thoughts. Remember, when you make an agreement with a thought, *it becomes a belief.* On the following page you will see a template for this agreement. You can use this one, or make one of your own. Think about your new positive thoughts that honor your body and support your goals and dreams. When you are finished, sign this agreement with those thoughts so that they can become empowering beliefs. After you have signed it, keep it in a special place somewhere, maybe in your personal journal; or even frame it and hang it on your bedroom wall so that you can remind yourself every morning that you have made this agreement to have positive beliefs.

My Contract to Honor My Body And Soul

I, _____, have broken any and all agreements with negative thoughts and will now replace them with the following positive thoughts in regard to my physical, emotional and spiritual body:

_____
_____
_____
_____

I am aware that by making this agreement, I am providing these positive thoughts with

the strength to become new, empowering beliefs. I am further aware that it is these new

beliefs that will assist me in healing and, in turn, achieving all of my goals and dreams.

Dated this _____ day of _____, 20____

Signature: _____

day 7: free write

TODAY'S AFFIRMATION: *I release the shadows of my past and free myself from the fear of the unknown.*

TODAY IS A 'FREE WRITE'. Write about any feelings you had while completing this week's exercises. Were there any surprises? What did you learn about yourself? How did you do with this week's Challenge? Feel free to write about anything and everything that comes into your head. Get it out, free your mind, put it on the paper.

Sandy Lynn

Complete this statement: I AM

step 3: give to yourself

"You are allowed to be both a masterpiece and a work in progress simultaneously."
Sophia Bush

TO THIS POINT, we've been working hard on dissecting and letting go of negative thoughts. Now we get to rebuild. Just like renovating a house, it's hard work to take it all apart and rip it down to the studs, but the great part is that you can rebuild it into a castle. When you have self limiting beliefs though, it's like you're trying to build your castle on sand. Those negative waves keep coming and knocking down what you're trying to build. It's a constant battle. But, if we can move away from the sand and build on solid ground, which is our positive beliefs, then the waves can't tear it down and our castle can stand strong.

Last week we talked about self-acceptance. As we move into ***Step 3–Give to Yourself***, I would like to talk to you about responsibility. I can learn to accept the fact that I'm overweight or middle aged, or my nose is too big, or whatever. That's the self acceptance part. But if I want to make changes, that's where self-responsibility comes in. We are each responsible for taking care of our own healing. You can choose to keep fighting the waves that tear down your sand castle, or you can do the work and build your foundation on solid ground. This is the hardest part–it's almost harder than self-acceptance. And no one else can do it for you. It's so easy to feel sorry for yourself; to sit around and complain about how bad your life is. But, if you're not going to take the responsibility to do something about it, it's never going to change. In fact, it will probably get worse. Every person has responsibility over their own well-being and the health of their own internal state. That's because no one outside of you has any power over you unless you *choose* to give it to them. Reading this book and doing the necessary work so far, means that you have chosen to take your power back. You are accepting responsibility for your own healing.

When I look back on my life, I realize that the hardest times that I've had, the times that I felt the worst both mentally and physically, were times that I gave up my power. To be honest, until about 5 years ago, I almost never stood in my own power, but I didn't recognize that. There was a period of about 5 years when I was doing very well. I had been single for a while, I had quit smoking, I felt good about my weight; so I decided to try dating again. I had a few 'disaster dates', but then….I met the man who (at the time) I thought was my soul mate. The first time we met we were communicating without words and finishing each other's sentences. It felt as if we were almost the same person. Within a month he was telling me that he loved me; and begging me to 'let him in' to my heart. I was a little 'gun shy' and I knew it was too soon to be having such strong feelings but I couldn't deny them. I decided to let my guard down and let things take their course. For 6 months I was happier than I had been in a very long time. So happy that I ignored every single red flag. I allowed him to control the relationship because I was afraid it would end and I would lose this happy feeling. Finally, I came to a point where I couldn't ignore the flags and I had to accept that he was cheating.

My life fell apart. I was devastated. I couldn't get out of bed for weeks except to go to work, and even then I was like a zombie. I don't even remember most of the next few months. I ended up in such a depression that I lost my job, I gained weight. I also dated…a lot. I could not fathom the idea that he had cheated on me so I was bound and determined to move on. But it didn't help. What also didn't help was that he realized his new relationship wasn't all he had hoped and he would call me now and then. Most often he would call after he found out that I had been on a date. He would call me and tell me that none of my dates would ever go well because he and I were supposed to end up together. The crazy thing was that I loved these phone calls… he must still care about me if he's calling because he's jealous… right?

I would love to be able to tell you that eventually I stopped answering his calls and that I moved on, but I can't. I cannot explain the hold that this man had over me. We ended up being friends. Strictly platonic, he was still dating the woman he had cheated on me with and I was going out on dates as well. I even gave him relationship advice. His relationship ended. I stopped dating. But we were still just friends. When the COVID pandemic hit we ended up spending a lot of time together. He lived just a couple of blocks away from me and he became a part of my 'bubble', one of a limited number in my social circle. We spent almost every evening together. He taught me how to play darts and we talked to each other about anything and everything; we shared our deepest darkest secrets with each other. He was my best friend. He often said that he loved me but he knew he wasn't in a mindset to be in a relationship. I still had very strong feelings for him as well. Everyone thought we were a couple. I guess it was what you would call a situationship.

Not long after the pandemic ended, he asked me if I would consider giving him another chance. It had been two years since he cheated on me. We spent all of our free time together. Neither one of us really spent time with anybody else. We were best friends. I could not explain this connection. I was convinced he was my twin flame. Maybe we were meant to be together after all. How could it not work out? We had spent every day together for the last two years. After a couple of days of thinking about it I decided that I wanted nothing more than to try again. We were so happy. We made so many plans. That lasted about six months. Then I noticed him pulling away again, and again I ignored the red flags. I knew what was happening and I chose not to see it. It was easier for me to pretend it wasn't happening than to admit that I, an intelligent and beautiful woman, had been played again. Eventually his best friends told me that they had seen him with another woman; and I went through the roller coaster all over again.

That was 3 years ago. It took a long time for me to get past it. In fact, I still often think about the 'what ifs'. I really beat myself up about it. I felt like such a fool for letting it happen again. Fool me once shame on you, fool me twice shame on me, right? Then I realized that the only way I was going to get past this was to stop feeling sorry for myself and take responsibility for my own healing. Slowly I began to realize that I was no longer waiting to hear his text tone. I no longer feel the butterflies when he texts me and tells me he misses me. I used to respond immediately if he did text me but I don't do that anymore. I have finally come to a point where I have taken back control. It was a hard lesson to learn but I have learned it very thoroughly, and I will never give anyone that power again.

Have you, or are you, giving anyone else control of your life, your emotions, your happiness? Think hard about that. Do you make decisions based on what you want? On what is best for you? Or do you make decisions that will make someone else happy? Or out of fear? A lot of this is because our Inner Child still needs to feel loved, no matter what; or because of his or her need for approval. Do you have a problem setting boundaries? Or saying 'no' to people? In this part of our journey we are going to take back our power. It's time to learn how to Give To Yourself.

week 6: healing your inner child

"Wherever you go, no matter what the weather, always bring your own sunshine."
Anthony J. D'Angelo

HAVE you ever had an argument with someone and afterward you just curled up in a ball and cried? Or have you ever had someone be mean to you and felt your rebellious teenager come forward, wanting to retaliate? This is your **Inner Child.** We have all had at least one childhood experience where we didn't get the love, or the response, that we needed at the time. Some of us more than others. The thing is, there's an illusion of adulthood, but most adults are wounded children in grownup bodies. We can see evidence of this all around us on full display. Sometimes in a personal context with ourselves and in our relationships; but also on a larger display in politics, in business, etc. Think about some celebrity figures like Britney Spears or Amanda Bynes. These are individuals who are dealing with a damaged Inner Child which has resulted in behavior that we would not expect from most adults. Political figures who behave extremely inappropriately or violent individuals who have not mastered self-regulation; these are all examples of people who have not healed their Inner Child. For most of us, if our Inner Child acts out because of insecurity or fear, it only affects those closest to us. If you're a public figure, on the other hand, your Inner Child acting out can cause world events and major messes, because we have wounded 3 year olds running the show. Imagine if these people had healed Inner Children. How would they show up in the world?

For me it has been a difficult but very rewarding journey going back and dissecting every aspect of my behavior: how I respond to people, the relationships I've had, and figuring out why I feel the way I feel and handle things the way I do. I talked a lot in the introduction to this book about my journey and what it felt like to realize how broken I was, but I also want to stress how rewarding it is. My life has changed so much! I am doing what I want to do, and I am doing it with confidence. I only need the approval of myself. Someone once told me that constantly looking for external validation is like a sugar high. It feels so great for a short amount of time, but eventually you will crash. I'm not saying I never crash anymore, my Inner Child still needs encouragement and reassurance and a hug or two once in a while. But now I am at the point where I can recognize what it is that she needs and take care of it right away, so my 'crashes' happen much less frequently and they don't last anywhere near as long.

At the beginning of this journey we did some work with your Inner Bully. We looked into what he or she sounded like, looked like, and where the voice might be coming from. Now that we have quieted that bully it's time to get to know your Inner Child; that little one inside of you that has been begging for your attention. It is time to find out what they need. It's time to give them what they have been missing all of this time. You may know some of this already; you may not. You may be able to pinpoint or recall specific incidents from your childhood that have done some emotional damage or left you with some trauma. Or you may not. Those specific details don't matter right now. What does matter is that you are ready, willing and open to listening. You must be prepared to be present and see yourself and some aspects of your life from a new perspective. I think that one of the hardest parts about healing is that you have to tear yourself down before you can build yourself back up. The 'you' that you have built thus far in your life…the one who is so strong, the one who never cries, the one who just keeps on going no matter how hard it gets…that is not the real 'you'. That 'you' was built out of necessity, out of fear, out of self-preservation. It is time to tear away that mask and re-parent your Inner Child. It is time to build the you that is fearless and ready to create the life that you have always wanted.

Weekly Challenge: Find a photo of yourself as a young child. If that is not possible, find something that can represent you as a child. Each day this week, before you start your day, before you meditate, before you go to sleep, look at this photo or this object and picture yourself at a young age. Speak to your Inner Child. Tell them you love them, that they are safe, and that it is okay to trust this process.

Weekly Meditation: Week 6–Acknowledging Your Inner Child

day 1: getting to know your inner child

TODAY'S AFFIRMATION: *My Inner Child's voice deserves to be heard.*

I AM GOING to be honest with you…when I signed up for my first Breathwork session with Jay Bradley (who eventually became my mentor and my dear friend), he told me to bring a photo of myself as a young child. And when he told me that the reason I needed to bring it is so that I could connect with my Inner Child I thought "oh boy, is this for real?" On the day of the session, as we finished up the breathwork and prepared to meditate, Jay led me through some Ho'Oponopono. (I will tell you more about that a bit later). What Jay asked me to do was hug myself and tell myself 'I love you'. I have to admit that it was awkward and I felt a bit silly. But as I got to know more about myself and got to know my Inner Child, I realized how important this was. She had felt so unloved and so unsure of herself that she spent her entire life trying to please other people. So much so, that she put her own needs aside. The more I did it, the easier it got, and the stronger I felt. So as you go through this week, if you feel awkward or silly or uncomfortable, acknowledge those feelings. Use the 90 Second Rule and allow them to process and pass through your system; and then refocus on connecting with your Inner Child. As the saying goes: "Trust the process." It will be worth it.

Today you are going to start communicating with your Inner Child. After the 'Weekly Mediation', grab your journal and your childhood photo. With that child in mind, just start to write. See what they have to say. Write down any thoughts. Pay attention to your body's sensations (this is your Inner Child speaking to you). If it helps, you can ask questions like:

- How are you feeling today?
- Is there anything you want me to know?
- What do you need?

Just start the conversation and let the communication begin.

day 2: who created your beliefs?

TODAY'S AFFIRMATION: *My Inner Child deserves love, honor and respect.*

I ONCE HAD a therapist ask me about my inability to get angry. As I have said before, I was raised in a family that didn't show a lot of outward emotion. My reply to him was that I didn't feel that anger was useful. Once something has happened there is no point in wallowing in it or making it worse. Arguing with someone is not going to change what happened. I would rather be angry on my own and get over it on my own than have a confrontation and make things uncomfortable in the future. We continued on to have a discussion about how anger was an important emotion and that it was unhealthy to keep it inside.

Then he asked me about my relationship with my mother. I told him that she was an amazing mother. She took care of my little sister and I on her own without any help from my dad, and she never complained. He asked a lot of questions about family dynamics. I must have mentioned how I felt that my sister got more attention because she was the youngest. I talked about how

I didn't necessarily get along with my stepfather so I left home at 16. By the time I was 17, I was in a relationship with a man who was abusive. The therapist asked me if my mother ever intervened in or talked to me about the abuse. I explained to him that it wasn't in our family dynamic to interfere in each other's marriages or child-rearing. Then he asked me why I wasn't angry with my mother. That didn't go over well with me. In my eyes my mother was a saint. "Yes", he said, "but she also put everyone else's needs above yours. She favored your younger sister and gave her more attention and love. When the two of you had an argument she took your sister's side. She never stuck up for you when your stepfather treated you unfairly. When it came to getting love from her…you were at the bottom of the totem pole. I would be angry with her for that. Why aren't you?" I left his office feeling very angry with him. How dare he say those things about my mother.

It wasn't until years later, when I learned about my Inner Child and started to communicate with her, that I realized how important that conversation was. My mother was a wonderful person. She was kind and sweet and everyone loved her. And she was not, by any means, a bad mother. She was doing the best that she could in the situation that she was in with the tools that she had. I loved her very much. But that didn't change the fact that my Inner Child felt rejected, unloved and angry. I only wish I had learned all of this sooner, maybe it would have made a difference for my mom too.

- What are the three most important relationships in your life and how have they influenced your beliefs about yourself? Both positively and negatively.

- Now, take a deep breath, center yourself, go within and ask your Inner Child this same question. Listen carefully for the answers and acknowledge his/her feelings.

day 3: being aware of self-sabotage

TODAY'S AFFIRMATION: *I will give myself the grace and the time to heal my Inner Child.*

AT THE BEGINNING of this book we did a lot of work to quiet your Inner Bully. Before you start the healing process, there is a constant battle going on inside of you between your Inner Bully and your Inner Child. Through the process of healing, we strive to quiet your Inner Bully and make your Inner Child feel strong and loved and beautiful. The interesting thing about your Inner Bully, is that even though that bully seems to be beating your Inner Child into submission, oftentimes it is an act of protection. It's like that old saying, "What you don't know won't hurt you". Your bully is saying "if you don't try you can't get hurt". It reminds me of the old cartoons where there is a devil sitting on one shoulder and an angel sitting on the other, and the devil is speaking loud enough that the angel can't be heard. So when your Inner Child is thinking, 'I'm not good enough, I screw everything up, nothing works out for me'; that's a sign of self-sabotage. *If I convince myself that I'm not good enough, I won't* *even try; so there's no way I can fail.* Once you become aware of the battle going on inside of you, you're another step further in your healing process. The closer you get to self-love, the less you need the protection. Your Inner Bully gets quieter and quieter, and your Inner Child becomes stronger and more self-confident.

Signs of self-sabotage: Answer the following questions honestly. Give examples if you think of them.

- Are you a procrastinator?

- Have you ever not attempted something because you've already convinced yourself you can't do it?

- Have you ever said yes to something when you didn't really want to?

- Have you ever quit something when it became difficult?

- Have you ever started more projects than you can finish?

- Do you blame others when things go wrong?

- Do you stay in relationships that you know are not good for you?

- Do you put yourself down or use self-deprecating humor? (make jokes at your own expense)

Were you surprised at anything that came to your mind while you were answering these questions? Were you aware that you were doing this? What are some strategies you can use to quiet your Inner Bully/saboteur?

day 4: safe spaces

TODAY'S AFFIRMATION: *I am able to create a safe and welcoming environment for myself.*

WHEN I WAS A CHILD, my safe place was with my Mummu (Mummu is Finnish for grandmother). When I was with her I always felt seen and heard. When she hugged me, I knew that nothing bad could ever get to me. It was like I could feel the love radiating from her body into mine. When Mummu was around, she was my champion. She made sure that there was no favoritism. She spoke up when she felt I was being treated unfairly. She was my hero. I think one of the saddest days of my life was the day that we moved out of the house that was right next to hers. Even as I got older and became an adult, she was the person that I went to when I needed to feel grounded and safe. To me, she was a soulmate, and the day that she died, a huge piece of my heart died with her. It's been 17 years now since I lost her, and I still miss her every day.

As we get older, we often lose our 'safe spaces', and we forget about how important they are. Many of us think of our bedrooms as our sacred space, a place where we can escape the outside world and come back to our selves. This can work well for some people; but in reality the bedroom is often a place where the bed is unmade, there may be clothes on the floor and baskets of laundry that we haven't gotten to yet. Some of us have bedrooms that double as offices, or we do a lot of work on our laptops while in bed. It is so important that we create a space for ourselves that has *no outer distractions.* A place where we can sit comfortably and just forget about that laundry, that paperwork, or those dishes and just nurture our Inner Child. A place where our 'fight or flight' instincts can be turned off and we feel relaxed and comfortable and safe; where we can release our emotions without judgment. Even if it's just for a few minutes a day.

This was something that clearly hit home for me when my adult daughter moved back home with her boyfriend. It was difficult to find a place of my own. Yes, I had a bedroom, but, due to necessity, it also became my office space. I realized that I really needed a safe space to relax so I turned a corner of my bedroom into a quiet space for meditating, reading, or anything else that didn't involve house chores or work. It didn't take much, I bought some very inexpensive sheers and made a canopy so I couldn't see what didn't need to be seen. A bunch of throw pillows on the floor, a soft blanket, all in shades of my favorite colors. A little shelf for candles, sage, the current book I was enjoying or tarot cards and I had a beautiful little space to just 'unplug' for a few minutes.

Take a few deep breaths and center yourself. Connect with your Inner Child. Think back to your childhood:

- As a child, where was it that you felt the most safe?

- Did you have a 'safe space'? Describe it? What made it your safe space?

- How does remembering it make you feel?

- Do you have a 'safe space' as an adult? How could you create one?

day 5: most of your sh*t didn't start with you

TODAY'S AFFIRMATION: *I am in control of my thoughts and energy.*

THERE IS a theory in sociology called 'The Looking Glass Self Theory'. The idea behind it is that we base our self-esteem and our feelings of self-worth on how we *think* other people view us. We try to mold ourselves (our clothing, physical appearance, makeup etc.) in a way that we believe will please those around us. We perceive how others see us and that sets the basis for how we feel about ourselves. Unfortunately, our perceptions are often skewed by our life experiences and how we have been taught to see ourselves during childhood. We can never know exactly how someone else sees us, but we are really good at making things up in our minds based on past relationships. For example, when I was cheated on, I made the assumption that the other woman must have been prettier than I was, or skinnier than I was, or sexier than I was. I had, since childhood, believed that I wasn't good enough, so this train of thought fit right in with the way I already felt about myself. It led me to believe that others saw me as fat and ugly, and so, that's the way I began to view myself. When I was able to go back in to see that relationship from a healing perspective, I was able to see that it had nothing to do with me and everything to do with him. I was able to see myself from a different perspective, and the 'Looking Glass Self' started to fade. I was seeing myself from my own perspective.

The question I posed to you on Day 1 was: *What are the three most important relationships in your life and how have they influenced your beliefs about yourself? Both positively and negatively.* Think about your answer to that question. When we talked about your Inner Bully we released any negativity that stems from past relationships. Remind yourself that the burden you are carrying comes from them, not you. Your Inner Child needs to let go too.

- Go back to the Weekly Meditation and think about the things that you and your Inner Child have been working on releasing. Write them below, then write about who you may have gotten them from and why. Again, remind yourself that the burden is not yours to carry. Are you both ready to let it go?

day 6: make it right

TODAY'S AFFIRMATION: *My light is bright enough to cast out darkness.*

THE FIRST TIME I practiced Breathwork I was also introduced to a spiritual practice called Ho'Oponopono. The term is a Hawaiian word that loosely translated means "to make right", Ho'Oponopono is a healing practice that allows us to forgive not only ourselves but other people, or even things or situations that are causing us to remain a victim. It teaches that holding blame only compounds the problem, and it is important to forgive as holding on to these feelings or memories can affect our everyday life. The idea is that if we can take responsibility not only for ourselves, but for others' who have hurt us as well, we are taking responsibility for our own healing. In turn, we take back our power because we also then have the power to forgive,and we no longer feel powerless over our situation.

To practice Ho'Oponopono, all you need to do is find a quiet space to relax and connect with whatever or whoever your higher power is (the universe, source, God, Mother Earth). Reflect on the problem (or person) you are facing and how you are being affected. Be prepared to accept your responsibility for what has happened and be prepared to forgive all parties and move forward with love. You can speak to yourself, your Inner Child, a parent, your Inner Bully, money, even a body part that is troubling you.

Repeat the following phrases (in order), examples of what you might say if you are speaking to your Inner Child are written in brackets.:

- **"I love you"** (I love you so much)
- **"I'm sorry,"** (I'm sorry for being hard on you, for all of your pain, etc.)
- **"Please forgive me,"** (for not always being there for you, etc.)
- **"Thank you,"** (for being so strong, for not giving up on me, etc)

Today we are going to practice Ho'Oponopono with your Inner Child. On the next page, next to the 4 Ho'Oponopono phrases write specific examples of what you would want to say to your Inner Child specifically. Then, follow the steps listed above. Ideally, you will repeat each phrase over and over until any negative or resistant energy starts to release.

Take some time afterward to journal about any feelings, memories or situations that may have come up for you.

I strongly suggest using this practice regularly, (even daily, in the 'safe space' you create for yourself).

Ho'Oponopono For My Inner Child:

"I love you…"

"I'm sorry…"

"Please forgive me…"

"Thank you…"

day 7: free write

TODAY'S AFFIRMATION: *I am my own hero.*

TODAY IS A 'FREE WRITE'. Write about any feelings you had while completing this week's exercises. Were there any surprises? What did you learn about yourself? How did you do with this week's Challenge? Feel free to write about anything and everything that comes into your head. Get it out, free your mind, put it on the paper.

Sandy Lynn

Complete this statement: I AM

week 7: reparent yourself so you can live in the present

"Do the best you can until you know better. Then when you know better, do better."
Maya Angelou

WHEN I WAS YOUNGER, my mom often would say with a big sigh, "Oh, Sandy, you're just like your father." Young Sandy, especially teenage Sandy, was okay with that; because I thought my dad was a rock star! My dad was a drummer in a band and he liked loud music and he was cool. Then I got older and I realized that in actuality he was an absent father who suffered from Peter Pan Syndrome. In my head, I still carried that message: "You're just like your father", and now it held a whole new meaning. A lot of that held me back – that simple comment. When I realized that maybe it wasn't so great to be just like my dad, I stopped dreaming about being a singer. When it came to parenthood, I was really hard on myself to make sure that my kids were given everything they needed. I was obsessed with doing the right things as a parent. Was I giving them enough attention? Was I treating them equally? A lot of my insecurities about parenting stemmed from that one little phrase. I did not want to be like my dad. Sometimes it's just the littlest things that people say to you as a child that stay with you and you carry it with you for a lifetime.

When I started to think about it, I began to realize that there were so many things that I carried forward from my childhood that were holding me back from living my life to the fullest. The shame I felt that came from my mom, the abandonment issues that I had because of my father's actions, and all of the little phrases and situations that made me feel so small were still my burdens at almost 50 years of age. Living in these past experiences kept me frozen as the child I was raised to be, rather than the adult that I was meant to become. I had to re-parent myself to learn to be myself in the present moment rather than a ghost of the past. By doing this, I was choosing myself. I was telling myself that I didn't need to be anywhere, do anything, or be anyone else in order to be whole. I was rewriting my story, and that became my motto: "My story starts right now."

The past and the future don't exist except in your mind, so why live there? Last week we talked about how to connect with your Inner Child, how to recognize and acknowledge the feelings of your Inner Child. So now, if we can move into living in the present moment all the time, we won't constantly be falling back into that habit of reacting out of pain. We won't continue to live in a state of victimhood. Holding on to the past keeps us from being able to show up in the present moment with love. It's also important to remember that you don't have to have been through a crazy, traumatic, abusive childhood to be damaged. Just a small, misguided statement from a significant adult (a parent, a teacher, a coach, or anyone else that you respect) can affect you deeply. Everybody has something in their past that needs to be rewritten, because believe it or not, unhealthy parenting is actually not that uncommon.

You can only find yourself in the present moment–not in the past, not in the future. You are real only in *this* moment. We imprison ourselves by living in our past. We build cages of limitations by holding on to our judgments of who we were and what we've done or our judgments of others. When you become present, you can finally access and accept the real you and stop keeping score. By taking some time to reparent yourself, you can begin releasing stories, judgment, decisions you've made about yourself and others. Through reparenting, you allow your Inner Child to grow up into a new person. Not limiting him or her with your ideas of the past.

Weekly Challenge: Go back to your childhood. Be a kid again. Remember the things that you loved to do: color, write stories, watch cartoons, put your toes in the mud, walk barefoot in the grass. Make time to play every day this week, even if it's just for a few minutes. Let yourself feel inspired and creative again.

Weekly Meditation: Week 7–Putting Down Everything That's Not Yours to Carry

day 1: it's ok to be a kid sometimes

TODAY'S AFFIRMATION: *It is safe for me to laugh and play.*

WHEN I WAS little I wanted to be a ballet dancer, but we didn't have money for lessons. I also wanted to be a singer and sing in my dads band, but that was completely discouraged by my mom. My mom was a single parent, my dad didn't pay child support, and we had to try and get by on only her paycheck. My sister and I got used to going without all of the extra material things that a lot of our friends had. Now that I am an adult, I am doing the things that I wanted to do as a little girl. I'm taking a dance class–it's not ballet but it's still a dance class. I am also getting my singing in by taking musical theater. I try to be silly and do "kid" things as often as I can. It may not be perfect, but I am acknowledging the needs of my Inner Child.

- Make a list of things you loved to do as a child, or that you wish you could have done. You can use some of the things on this list for your challenge.

- Is there a toy or a game or an activity that you really wanted but for whatever reason you couldn't have it? (a certain doll, an art set, Disneyland? For me it was an Easy Bake Oven). Communicate with your Inner Child. How did/does he or she feel about it?

If you have the means, get that toy or have that experience with your Inner Child. Have some fun! Remember how to play!

day 2: recognizing parenting fails

TODAY'S AFFIRMATION: *I am an adult and I have the power to reparent myself.*

EVERYTHING that you experience in childhood sets up how you feel about yourself as an adult. The early years are a critical period of development, and what you receive, or don't receive, from the significant adults in your life will have a huge effect on your self-confidence and self-worth. These relationships will affect the way you navigate adult relationships. The way that you were parented will most likely affect the way that you deal with difficult emotions and situations as an adult.

- What needs did you miss out on as a child? Were they physical, emotional, social, or psychological?

- Are you able to see how this affects you as an adult? Explain.

day 3: stop blaming yourself

TODAY'S AFFIRMATION: *I feel safe in expressing myself as my adult self.*

A HUGE PART of re-parenting your Inner Child is the ability to stand back in the moment and recognize if what you're feeling is coming from your adult perspective, or your hurt Inner Child's point of view. This will help you to learn what coping methods you have been utilizing in order to soothe yourself. For example, I had no idea that my inability to ask for or accept help in any situation was a coping skill that I had developed. I saw it as being strong; showing everyone that I could handle things on my own. What it really was though, was my feelings of unworthiness coming through. I didn't feel that I deserved anyone's help. I didn't want to be a burden, and I really didn't want to owe anybody anything. It's really important that we learn to see these coping skills as a temporary crutch. By using them we may feel better for a little while. It may mask what we are truly feeling underneath, but eventually your body and mind become exhausted from constantly using these band aid solutions. Learn to see who you truly are, and what it is that you really need.

- When something goes wrong for you, or you feel that you are stuck in an uncomfortable situation, what is your reaction? Do you immediately take the blame? Do you try to avoid blame at all costs? Do you overreact or have trouble speaking up for yourself?

- Now ask yourself, are these emotions coming from the adult you; or the scared, damaged, Inner Child you?

day 4: you to the rescue!

TODAY'S AFFIRMATION: *I am thankful for the difficult lessons I have learned.*

ONE OF THE hardest things for me to learn, which has also been the most helpful, was to stop thinking about negative events in my life solely as negative events. What I mean by that is, I became familiar with the saying: "Stop asking why this is happening TO you and start thinking about why it's happening FOR you." When I started to think about it I realized that every 'bad' event or situation that I have experienced–break ups, losing jobs, losing friendships–they all had some kind of positive effect. I started to think about these events less as punishments and more as lessons.

For example, I told you a story about a relationship I had experienced that hurt me to the core. I used to be so embarassed to tell that story because I could not believe that I had allowed myself to be taken advantage of twice. When I think back on it now, there were telltale signs that it wasn't going to work…ever. Unfortunately, I just could not comprehend the idea that anyone could hurt and betray another person like that, especially more than once. I realize now that I needed to experience that relationship, that betrayal and hurt and embarrassment, because when all was said and done and I had come out the other side I knew that I would never allow that to happen to me again. I had learned, finally, that I was an amazing person. It was essentially the 'straw that broke the camel's back'. It was the beginning of my journey to healing. I knew what I wanted and I deserved better. That was one of the first steps to healing old wounds and breaking old habits.

Today I would like you to recall an event or memory from your childhood that fed into the negative beliefs that you have about yourself today. An event that 'scarred' your Inner Child that he or she still carries today. Try not to dwell on anything that may trigger you enough that you become overwhelmed and don't let yourself become too immersed in the memory.

- Write about the memory from your Inner Child's perspective. What was he or she feeling at that moment?

- Now, imagine yourself as an adult coming to the rescue. What would your adult self say to your Inner Child self?

- Help your Inner Child to reframe their thinking about themselves. What kind of person might they be if they had a rescuer back then? How might this have changed their feelings about themselves as they became an adult?

You just wrote the kind of person you want to be…the kind of person you will be now that you believe in yourself. Seeing the past from a different perspective will help you to break free from those negative memories that are holding you back.

day 5: reparenting

TODAY'S AFFIRMATION: *I am the hero in my own story.*

I LOVED MY MOM; but I didn't get what I needed from her; especially after she met my stepfather. He and I did not get along and I often felt that she sided with him. When I was about 10 years old I started to daydream that I was adopted and that my real family found me and took me home with them. I was their only child because they couldn't have imagined having any other children after me. I felt loved all the time and they always put me first and we lived happily ever after. Sometimes I imagined that my dad came to get me and he decided that he wanted me to live with him all the time. He taught me how to play the drums and let me sing with his band and everybody loved me. Our minds will do subtle little things when we are hurting to help us escape. I remember being jealous of my friends and their relationships with their fathers, or the opportunities that they were offered or the things they were encouraged to do. I still wonder sometimes what my adult self might have been like; how my path might have unfolded differently if I had been raised differently.

Today you are going to re-parent yourself. Write about your ideal parents. Maybe you have a favorite set of parents from a TV show or movie; or maybe you think of the parents of one of your friends growing up. What would your life have been like if they had been your parents, your role models? Think of specific events or examples in your life and how they might have handled things differently.

This is the kind of parent that you need to be for your Inner Child right now. Be the parent you didn't have so that you can change your perspective. What's stopping you?

day 6: be the parent you didn't have

TODAY'S AFFIRMATION: *I am the one who saves myself.*

TODAY YOU ARE GOING to write a letter to your Inner Child. In this letter you will tell him or her everything that they (you) needed to hear as a child. Maybe they need to hear how loved they are, or that they are safe, or that it is ok to express their emotions. Apologize for the wrongs that were done to them, or for the things they had to experience, or didn't get to experience. You can use the Ho'Oponopono phrases as a guide if you like. Finish off the letter by telling your Inner Child that you are ready to start a new story and that you are no longer going to repeat the mistakes and negative habits of the past. End on a positive, loving note.

day 7: free write

TODAY'S AFFIRMATION: *With every breath I honor who I am.*

TODAY IS A 'FREE WRITE'. Write about any feelings you had while completing this week's exercises. Were there any surprises? What did you learn about yourself? How did you do with this week's Challenge? Feel free to write about anything and everything that comes into your head. Get it out, free your mind, put it on the paper.

Sandy Lynn

Complete this statement: I AM

week 8: releasing codependency

"Be who you are and say what you feel, because those who mind don't matter and those who matter don't mind."
Dr. Seuss

ALL OF MY life I have put other peoples' needs ahead of my own. I was a people pleaser...with my family, my friends, and especially in my romantic relationships. I needed to feel needed. I needed people to like me. This was all at the cost of my own needs and wants, and sometimes at the cost of my own physical safety. When I was 17 I met a man who was much older than I was. I was in a place in my life where I felt like I didn't really have a home. I left my mom's because I wasn't getting along with my stepfather and moved in with my dad and his girlfriend. I left my dad's because his girlfriend had a mental illness and during one of her episodes, she and I had an awful fight. I was kind of floating, looking for my place. This man came in and convinced me that he would take care of everything. He treated me like I was special. He made me feel loved. We created a home together. He bought me an engagement ring and we got married just after my 19th birthday. I just knew that my fairytale was going to come true.

The first time he hit me I was so shocked that I had no idea what to do. We were out with some friends and someone cracked a joke at his expense. Everyone laughed, so did I, so did he; but after the laughter died down and no one was paying attention he cuffed me across the back of the head because I laughed. No one else noticed, or if they did they didn't say anything. I should have packed my bags that night, but when he sobered up he begged for forgiveness and told me he couldn't live without me. So I stayed, because he needed me, and I needed to be needed. This pattern continued for four years. Four years of being hit, pushed, dragged by my hair, and called awful names. Four years of bruises, black eyes and lies. I covered the abuse well, and when someone did figure it out I made excuses for him. I did not recognize the fact that I continued to stay with a partner who was bad for me because I needed him to help me to feel all the things that I had not learned to feel for myself. When you grow up feeling inadequate and unwanted, you become a 'helper'. You make yourself into what the other person needs because you become so dependent on those 'breadcrumbs' that come in between the episodes of abuse. I am so thankful that I had good friends who almost literally dragged me out of that relationship, or I don't know how long I would have stayed or what would have happened to me.

When I look back I can see how I followed the same pattern with my children's father. When we met, we were both very damaged. We found the things that we needed in each other. That's why we stayed together for so long. I want to emphasize that there was a lot of love in this relationship, and so much respect. The problem was that we were not able to heal individually as long as we were together, because we each played into each other's wounds. That was a big part of my marriage falling apart. I went back to school at his encouragement, and I started to become more independent and realized that I was intelligent and could be successful. As you start to heal, those things that you looked for or depended on are not needed as much, and the treatment that you once tolerated starts to feel unacceptable. After 20 years of me always being there for whatever he needed, suddenly I had school, meetings, assignments, projects and I wasn't there to do everything. As I grew more confident and started to speak up, he became more insecure in our relationship. It became a vicious cycle, and eventually we agreed that it was probably best to separate so that we both had time to think about what we wanted. I often look back and wish that we could have recognized the issues and the need for healing much sooner; maybe we could have made it work.

Unfortunately, those of us who didn't have the best childhood have this horrible need to be needed. This validates our worth. We find it difficult to leave relationships, even if the desire to end the relationship is mutual or comes from us. I've continued to talk with men I have ended relationships with for months because they continued to express how much they loved and needed me. Even after a breakup I was putting their needs ahead of my own. So, when it's the other person that breaks off the relationship it is devastating. I've had two relationships in my life where the other person has broken up with me. One was my very first love when I was 15 years old. The second one was with the man who cheated on me. Those events almost crippled me, because inside my Inner Child was screaming, "Why don't you like me? I tried so hard to be perfect. I did everything I was supposed to do. How can you turn your back on me?"

The term 'codependency' has been used more and more in recent years. I really had no idea what it meant at first, but as I learned more about it, I knew that it definitely described me. All of the characteristics that I have just described above are signs of codependency: putting others' needs ahead of your own, constant self-sacrifice, a fear of rejection, among others. I can see how this has been passed down from generation to generation through the women of my family. I can see that the example was set for me through watching my mother in her relationships. She set no boundaries and was extremely passive. It wasn't until she was much older that she started to live more for herself. In all of the reading I have done in regards to codependency, I pretty much checked every box.

The good news is that codependency is something that you can overcome. It takes work, but by completing this journal you have already begun a lot of this work. The main thing is that you have recognized that you have to take responsibility for your own healing. You are the only one that you can depend on for your own happiness. You have been getting to know who you really are, and learning what your own personal needs and wants are. This week we will continue with that process by talking about boundaries and how to establish them, which will assist you in releasing codependency.

Weekly Challenge: Spend at least 10 minutes each day practicing some sort of self care; doing something that you enjoy that is just for you. (Other than reading this book). Examples might be: a hot bath, a meditative walk, sitting and listening to your favorite music.

Weekly Meditation: Week 8–This is Me

day 1: recognizing co-dependency

TODAY'S AFFIRMATION: *My feelings and needs are valid and deserve to be acknowledged. It took me many, many years to realize that I was affected by codependency. I didn't even really know what it meant.*

FOR TODAY'S JOURNAL EXERCISE, think carefully about the following questions/statements. Answer them as honestly as you can, and give examples that you can remember.

- Do you avoid arguments at all costs or say nothing during an argument?

- Do other peoples' opinions of you really matter to you? Are their opinions more important than your own?

- Have you ever lived with someone who has/had issues with substance abuse?

- Have you ever been in a relationship with someone who physically or emotionally abused you?

- Do you have difficulty expressing your emotions?

- Do compliments or gifts make you uncomfortable?

- Do you ever feel 'less than' or doubt your value/ability?

- Do you have a hard time asking for help?

- Do you have a hard time saying 'no' when others ask you for help, even if you are already feeling overloaded?

- Do you feel responsible for everybody else in your life?

- Do you feel guilty for things that are not your fault?

How do you feel about your answers to these questions? Did anything surprise you? What does this tell you about yourself?

day 2: the importance of boundaries

TODAY'S AFFIRMATION: *I deserve a relationship that respects and values my individuality.*

I THINK that setting boundaries was one of the hardest things for me to learn. I didn't even realize that I didn't have boundaries. In my mind I was just being a good person, helping other people. It didn't even dawn on me that I was letting other people take advantage of me. I was trying to see the good in people, I could not see that I was not only allowing myself to be mistreated but I was enabling them at the same time. I had to learn that being selfish is okay. I had to learn that there was no reason for me to feel guilty for standing up for myself. Why was I enabling other people to feel good by putting my own needs aside?

It is important to remember that issues with boundaries do not occur only in your romantic relationships. When you have issues with codependency and trouble setting boundaries, you have them in all of your relationships: family, coworkers, employers, friends. Maybe you have a family member that you allow to belittle you. Maybe your coworker leaves you with the bulk of the work because they know you will just do it without complaining. Maybe your boss expects you to put in extra time without compensation. Or maybe you have a friend who talks and talks incessantly about their own problems but never has time to hear about yours. No matter what the relationship, in order to truly heal you need to leave behind the codependency and begin to live for yourself. This starts with realizing that you need to set boundaries and taking the steps to follow through. Setting and communicating your boundaries is your responsibility. Not only do you have to set those boundaries, but you need to communicate them in a way that makes it clear to the other person.

Today I want you to think about the relationships in your life. Knowing what you know about codependency and your own traits, answer the following questions:

- Can you see codependency in your current relationships?

- How can you set boundaries in your codependent relationships?

- How can you communicate these boundaries in a loving, compassionate, and firm way?

- How can you stick to your boundaries?

day 3: sometimes you have to walk away

TODAY'S AFFIRMATION: *I value and protect my time and energy.*

WHEN I ACTUALLY STARTED SETTING BOUNDARIES SOME of the people in my life had a really hard time with it. Many of them tried to make me the villain, saying that I had changed, that I was acting like I thought I was better than they were. The truth is that I *had* changed. I was finally starting to recognize my value and stand up for myself. I wasn't allowing myself to be treated like a doormat anymore. I didn't think that I was better than anyone else; I just finally realized that I was important too. It was hard for people to accept that I wasn't just going to say yes to whatever they asked me to do anymore. When I finally started to speak up instead of sitting quietly and timidly, I was accused of being difficult. At this point it was up to me to decide how to reinforce these boundaries. In some cases, I was able to communicate my boundaries and they were respected. In other cases, I had to distance myself from those individuals who chose to ignore them.

The hardest changes for me to face were the changes within my marriage. Now again, I want to make clear that when we met, we were both damaged in many ways. Our relationship and its downfall were the result of changes in both of us, which was unfortunate because there was also much love and respect there. I have mentioned before that we were beginning to have issues as a couple; and how those issues were amplified when I returned to school. For our entire relationship I had been the 'yes' person. I never questioned any decision. I went along with the plans even if I disagreed. I allowed myself to be spoken down to, to be told to shut up, to be belittled about my weight, and I never said a word.

When I returned to school, my self-confidence went up and I started to realize that I did have a lot to contribute to this world. I started to stand up for myself. I started to voice my opinion. I started to speak up when I was feeling disrespected or taken for granted. My husband, with his own emotional damage, did not know how to handle this. In a large sense it wasn't his fault. He wasn't used to it and he didn't know how to respond. When you've lived with someone for years who agrees with you on pretty much everything and just accepts everything you say and do without question, it's very confusing when they suddenly develop a voice. And so, in his eyes I was becoming difficult to live with. He became convinced that I was unhappy in our marriage and must be having an affair, no matter what I said or did to prove otherwise. In the end, our issues began not only affecting us, but our children. I had to decide if I was going to continue to allow my boundaries to be crossed, or if I was going to end the relationship, no matter how difficult that would be.

- Are you prepared to stick to your boundaries, even if

it means you may have to leave some relationships behind, or at least 'on pause' for a while?

- What will you do when your boundaries are crossed or ignored?

- How will you reinforce the boundary?

day 4: learn to live in the present

TODAY'S AFFIRMATION: *I am the guardian of my personal boundaries and peace of mind.*

HAVE you ever had an uncomfortable conversation with someone and then afterward you thought to yourself, "I should have said this", or, "oh I wish I would've said that"? That used to happen to me all the time. I would lose sleep at night going over conversations or situations that literally happened 15 or 20 years in the past, beating myself up for what I didn't say or do at the time. When I learned to live in the present, that became less of a problem for me. The past is the past, and needs to be left there.

What are the things you feel you should be doing in order to prove your value?

Think of a situation/conversation that you repeat over and over in your head. Things you should have said in a situation… things you should have done. Can you voice to this person how you're feeling? Can you tell them that when they do this, it makes you feel a certain way? Write down what you might say.

If it's something from very far back in the past, or you cannot communicate with this person anymore, write it down anyway. Get it out of your head and let it go!

day 5: overcoming the 'shoulda coulda wouldas'

TODAY'S AFFIRMATION: *I create and maintain healthy connections by setting boundaries that foster respect, trust, and growth.*

SOMETIMES WHEN WE don't set and stick to proper boundaries, we get stuck carrying a heavy load of what my mom would call the *'Shoulda, Coulda, Wouldas'*. The *'Shoulda Coulda Wouldas'* live in the scared part of your brain that doesn't believe in yourself. What ends up happening is that we use these *'Shoulda, Coulda, Wouldas'* as excuses for why we did not follow our own dreams or do the things we really want to do in our lives. With me, for example, I would say things like: "Well maybe I *coulda* had some kind of singing career if I *woulda* had the support of my parents." Or, "I *shoulda* taken those singing lessons but my partner thought they were a waste of time and money." It's so much easier to blame others for the things that we missed out on in life. But here's the thing: Ultimately, at some point, we have to take the responsibility for our own lives and our own healing. I cannot continue to blame my upbringing and my life experiences for all of the things that have gone wrong in my life. It's definitely not an easy road, but once you start building on your self-acceptance, you realize that you really can accomplish whatever you set your mind to. Once you stop living according to others' judgment and realize that your judgment scale is the only one that matters, you become free to pursue your own goals in whichever way you choose.

- Think about your *'Shoulda Coulda Wouldas'*. How can you turn those "should haves" into 'dones'? – as in "I did it! I'm done! "

- How will your life look in a few years if you don't set these boundaries?

- How will your life change if you set these boundaries today?

day 6: those nasty little 'yeahbuts'

TODAY'S AFFIRMATION: *My boundaries are sacred, and saying no is a powerful act of self-care.*

THE *YEAHBUTS* LIVE in your brain right next to the *Shoulda Coulda Wouldas*. These are sneaky little creatures that sneak in and hold you back without you even knowing it. These are the entities that poke up their creepy little heads whenever you are ignoring your own needs and taking care of others' needs instead. The *Yeahbuts* are an excuse...a direct result of not being able to say 'no'. For example, your friend calls you and asks you why you weren't at the lake this past weekend. She remembered you saying you were looking forward to finally having a weekend getaway. Your answer is "*Yeahbut* my neighbor really needed help moving so I stayed in town to help her."

The *Yeahbuts* are also very good at making you feel guilty whenever you try to do something for yourself. They know exactly what thoughts to put into your head to make you feel selfish, or that your needs and wants aren't important. Weren't you going to take that writing course and start getting ready to write your book? *Yeahbut* I really shouldn't be taking that time away from my kids. It doesn't make sense for my husband to turn down overtime when he makes so much more money than I do. Or: *Yeahbut* it's probably just a waste of time because I really need to be working full time anyway; I could never take time off to write a book. That was just a silly dream.

Stop letting the *Yeahbuts* get in your way! To do this you first need to learn how to identify and meet your own needs–figure out what those needs are. A lot of people say that needs and wants are two different things. But I truly believe that that is not always the case. Sometimes, we want something so much that it becomes a necessity. It is needed in order to truly make your soul happy.

- Make a list of your needs and wants. Don't try to distinguish between the two or use any judgment. What do you WANT to do? What does your soul NEED?

- Can you think of anyone who you should be saying 'no' to? Are you able to begin to start saying 'no'?

day 7: free write

TODAY'S AFFIRMATION: *Respecting my own boundaries is essential for my growth.*

TODAY IS A 'FREE WRITE'. Write about any feelings you had while completing this week's exercises. Were there any surprises? What did you learn about yourself? How did you do with this week's Challenge? Feel free to write about anything and everything that comes into your head. Get it out, free your mind, put it on the paper.

Sandy Lynn

Complete this statement: I AM

week 9: set yourself up for success

"The greater danger for most of us lies not in setting our aim too high and falling short, but in setting our aim too low and achieving our mark."
Michelangelo

I HAVE TWO CHILDREN, a boy and a girl, 18 months apart in age. My son was always very logical and easy to reason with. He did what he was told, he asked for permission, and he communicated his needs well. Just before his second birthday I told him that maybe it was time to put the diapers away and just wear big boy underwear. He agreed, and that was it, he was toilet trained. He was a quiet soul, but you could always tell that his mind was very active and inquisitive. He thought things through very carefully. My daughter was the type of child who lived intensely in the moment, so much so that she would sometimes forget to eat or pee or put on a sweater when it was cold. She was a passionate child who would stand up for what she believed in and defend her opinions fiercely when she felt a situation was unfair. This was, and is, something that I admire greatly about her. Each child, though from the same two parents, had different traits, skills and strengths. As a parent, I had to acknowledge these two types of personalities, and realize that the same parenting techniques were not going to work for both of them.

Every child is unique. The tools that you would use for each child are going to be slightly different because they think differently and operate differently. Our individual healing journeys are also going to be just as diverse. It's easy enough for me to say to someone "do an exercise, and everything is going to turn out great!" But if you haven't developed the tools to ensure that you're successful, you're going to give up. I know this because I've given up a million times. I have been talking about writing a book since I was a teenager, and I did try. I started so many times…only to give up. I gave up because I had not learned which tools I needed to succeed. In fact, most of the time I was just setting myself up for failure. I had not learned how to get rid of the Shoulda Coulda Wouldas and the Yeahbuts. It wasn't until I started practicing Breathwork and learning more about myself and why I was the way that I was that I was able to build my toolkit.

One of the reasons that most people are not successful is because they're not looking for these tools in the right place. They're looking outside at the other people in their lives who have what they want and they are thinking, "I wish that I had the same opportunities as that person". They wish that they had the other person's tools. But setting yourself up for success requires a level of self-knowledge and self-acceptance that allows you to work WITH yourself rather than trying to force yourself into a predetermined box with predetermined expectations. The question is: How do you know you have the right tools to be successful? What *are* the right tools to be successful? For example, if you decide that you'd like to meditate every day, what tools would you need? You might be the type of person who needs to set up a physical meditation space. Maybe you need an accountability partner, or an alarm or an app or to block it off on your calendar. You have to start by getting to know yourself, your needs, your strengths. Then you can fill in the gaps and collect the resources, knowledge, and support that you need in order to set yourself up for success. The methodology is going to be different for each person. It's about you knowing yourself so you can do the thing YOU need to do in order to give yourself the opportunity to succeed.

Weekly Challenge: Let's work on a 'Beginners Bucket List'. Make a list of small things that you would like to accomplish. Maybe you would like to take a dance class, or speak in front of a group of people. A Bucket List doesn't have to be a list of huge, epic things. You don't need to climb Mount Everest. (Unless you want to, of course). Keep it simple for now. Even small steps in the direction you want to go are better than no steps at all.

Weekly Meditation: Week 9–My Needs Come First

day 1: achievement actions and harmful habits

TODAY'S AFFIRMATION: *Understanding my own personal success starts with understanding myself.*

WE ALL HAVE specific conditions that set us up for success. I like to call these *'Achievement Actions'*. These conditions are often linked to your behavior, habits, and beliefs. For example, I know that before I host a workshop or teach a class, I need to leave myself enough time to make several trips to the restroom. If I don't, then I have this underlying anxiety that I will get halfway through the workshop and I will have to go. For other people, they may feel that they need to make the bed as soon as they get out of it. These are just small examples, but they are reflections of bigger underlying beliefs that shape how you set yourself up for success. On the shadow side of this are our *'Harmful Habits'*. These are things that you do that can sabotage your success or get in the way. In my case I always find 'something more important to do'. For example, writing my book. I know that I should take the time to sit down and write, but isn't it more important for me to get that pile of laundry done? Usually, when our *'Harmful Habits'* surface, it's because there's an underlying fear or unresolved emotion that wants to be dealt with. I always thought of other things as 'more important' than writing my book because I didn't believe in myself. My Inner Bully was taking control.

When you get to know what your *'Achievement Actions'* and your *'Harmful Habits'* are, you are better able to recognize when you're doing–or not doing–the things that will set you up for success.

Think back to a time when you felt successful or extremely good about yourself. Write about it. Can you identify your 'Achievement Actions' in this case?

On the flip side of that, think about the times that you feel down or depressed or just not motivated at all. What 'Harmful Habits' crept in during these times?

day 2: using your tools

TODAY'S AFFIRMATION: *I take control of my actions and behaviors from this point forward.*

TAKE a look at what you wrote yesterday about your personal Achievement Actions and Harmful Habits. Start thinking more deliberately about the actions that you take–or don't take. One thing that I've noticed is that my Harmful Habits come out in full force when I'm self sabotaging. When the *Yeahbuts* and the *Shoulda Coulda Wouldas* come out to play my bedroom is a mess, I don't put things in their proper place, and I stop meditating regularly. My life falls into chaos. And when that happens I lose all motivation and get sucked into social media or streaming television.

It took me years to discover the bigger, underlying issues. For so many years my life was so programmed for taking care of others that when I no longer had to do that I was lost. So, I've come to understand that I am the type of person that needs a schedule. I need a program, but not someone else's program. I had to learn to make the schedule myself. One that allows me to pursue my wants and needs. Most of the time the schedule is actually written out and posted on my bedroom wall. At times, when I get really off track, I turn that schedule into a checklist for a couple of weeks to make sure I'm sticking to it. I also need to make sure that my environment is tidy and that everything is in its place; because for me, a DECLUTTERED SPACE allows for a DECLUTTERED MIND.

Today I would like you to go deeper into the daily behaviors that set you up for success, and define these behaviors more specifically. What else can you do to set yourself up for success today?

Make a list of all the various Achievement Actions that you need to take. These are your tools for success. Beside each item listed write about the bigger, underlying issue. Understanding what makes you tick and what kind of tools you need in your personal tool kit is one of the first steps to setting yourself up for success.

day 3: identify success spongers

TODAY'S AFFIRMATION: *I will let go of people and things that do not support my highest good.*

DO you have (or have you ever had) that friend that is so completely negative that you just feel exhausted and discouraged after spending time with them? That friend is a *'Success Sponger'*. That family member that never acknowledges your accomplishments or completely downplays them...*Success Sponger.* Anxiety, especially anxiety about things that haven't even happened yet....*Success Sponger.* And the biggest *Success Spongers* of all in today's society are all of the distractions that are available to us: Social Media, Television, Video Games. Statistics show that the average time spent on screens connected to the internet globally is 6 hours and 40 minutes a day (Revealing Average Screen Time Statistics 2025).

We all have *Success Spongers* in our lives. These are people, habits or behaviors that divert our energy into unproductive places. These *Success Spongers* will come into your energy field and try to soak up every bit of positive energy that flows through your body. They are able to find your weak points and your triggers and just drain you. The best way to stop a *Success Sponger* is to avoid it completely. Sometimes this is extremely hard to do. It's not always easy to cut a negative person out of our lives, especially if it is a family member. The most important thing then, is to become aware of the weaknesses and triggers that the *Success Spongers* are targeting. When we are aware then we can either remove or protect them so that the Spongers have nothing to latch on to.

Make a list of all of the *Success Spongers* in your life. Be brutally honest with yourself. As much as you love your best friend, is he or she a Success Sponger? Are you easily distracted? How much time do you spend online or staring at a screen (unnecessarily)? Now go over your list again and think about which triggers or weak spots these Spongers are targeting. How can you remove or protect them?

day 4: identify a specific goal

TODAY'S AFFIRMATION: *I am worthy of success.*

YOUR CHALLENGE this week was to start making a Bucket List of things you would like to accomplish. Today I would like you to start thinking about some specific goals. Again, they don't all have to be huge, epic goals. They can be as simple as: "I would like to lose 10 pounds", or "I would like to get a meditation space set up in my bedroom". Think about some bigger goals too. Things that you've always dreamed about doing that you just haven't gotten to, or even things that you might feel are out of reach. Once you have all of your goals written down, rate them in order from what you feel are the most easily attainable to the hardest to reach.

day 5: assembling the tools you need

TODAY'S AFFIRMATION: *I am capable of making my dreams a reality.*

CHOOSE a specific goal from yesterday's list. What tools and resources do you already use that help you create Achievement Actions? How do you set yourself up for success for that specific goal? What additional tools, resources, and support do you need to set yourself up for success?

On the flip side of that, what Harmful Habits and Success Spongers do you think will come forward for you as you try to achieve this goal? What will you do to protect yourself from these Harmful Habits?

day 6: set yourself up for success - breaking it down into smaller steps

TODAY'S AFFIRMATION: *I am motivated by my vision of success.*

IT'S time to set yourself up for Success! On the next page you will find a template for your Success Plan. (or you can download it from my website on the same page where you find the meditation recordings). This Success Plan is essentially a goal setting chart where you can take all of the things we've talked about this week and put them together and accomplish your goal.

Your Success Plan will include your:

- Achievement Actions and how you will foster them
- Harmful Habits and how you will avoid them
- Success Sponges and how you will stop them
- Any other tools or outside resources you might need
- A timeline for completing your goal

Once you have created your Success Plan it is up to you to

follow it! You know the tools that you have to work with and what you need to overcome any hurdles. You can do it! Hang it somewhere where you can see it every day. I usually hang mine on my bedroom wall so that I can see it every morning.

I Am...

My Success Plan

The Long Term Goal:

_____

(Note: SMART goals are Specific, Measurable, Achievable, Relevant and Time-bound)

Small, Measurable Steps (Break your goal down into baby steps so it's not overwhelming)	Achievement Actions (What are the actions that you need to take to set you up for success?)	Harmful Habits (What thoughts do I need to change in order to achieve my goal? How do I silence my Inner Bully?)	Success Sponges (What excuses, behaviours, people do I need to avoid in order to achieve my goal?)	Other Tools or Resources I May Need	Timeline and Evidence of Success (Realistic deadlines. What will tell me that I have been successful?)

day 7: free write

TODAY'S AFFIRMATION: *I have all of the skills that I need to achieve my dreams.*

TODAY IS A 'FREE WRITE'. Write about any feelings you had while completing this week's exercises. Were there any surprises? What did you learn about yourself? How did you do with this week's Challenge? Feel free to write about anything and everything that comes into your head. Get it out, free your mind, put it on the paper.

Sandy Lynn

Complete this statement: I AM

step 4: self gratitude!

> *"What we fear of doing most is usually what we most need to do."*
> *Ralph Waldo Emerson*

I LIVE in a part of the world where there is a lot of snow in the winter. Sometimes after a big snow, when my kids were little, we would go outside to play. They would love it when I walked in front of them in the deep snow and they could follow my footsteps, making it a little bit easier for them to get around. In a lot of ways this book is about getting ready to start your own journey so that you feel confident to stand on your own and stop traveling in someone else's footsteps. It's about feeling strong enough to make your own footprints, which means, you can go anywhere you want to go, and if there is no path you will make your own.

In my own journey, I had to stop worrying so much about what other people needed and what other people thought and just have faith in the fact that I was going to be okay no matter what.

Yes, I'm going to take these dance classes, and invest in

writing this book. Is it costing me and putting a big dent in my savings? Yes, but I'm doing what I want and need to do, and in the end it's going to be worth it. I know that there are people who are looking at me right now and wondering, "how is she doing this?" Thinking I'm crazy for turning down a full time contract in order to pursue my dreams. Wondering to themselves: "How is she supporting herself? Why is she wasting money on this or that?" The thing is, to me it's not a waste. I have become grateful to be the person that I am and, in turn, I have come to see that I deserve to have my needs fulfilled. I have also begun to see wants and needs in a different way.

There are the things that you need to survive; and there are the things that you need to make your soul happy. The rest are wants. Do I need a million dollars in order to survive? No. Do I need a million dollars to make my soul happy? No. Do I want a million dollars? Well, of course that would be nice. If I personalize this more…Did I need to write this book to survive? No. Did I need to write this book to make my soul happy? Yes! Everyone has different 'soul needs', and we have to sit quietly and really look inside of ourselves to find them. But they are so important, because if your soul is not happy and at peace then you are not really living, you are simply existing. So, I am paying attention to my 'soul needs'. I'm not going to a job that I hate everyday. I'm not coming home so defeated and exhausted that I'm sitting in front of a TV for five or six hours. I'm not dwelling on the negative, thinking about how the 'world is going to crap' and complaining about how the government is going to take over everything that we do. I am the only one who has control of my soul, so I don't care! I'm going to the lake. See you later! I'm going to talk to the birds. They are always happy.

When you let go of the need for approval from the outside, when you stop listening to all of the negative voices in your head, you start to realize that you are the writer of your own story, and you can restart your story at any time. You have been working on letting go of what is not needed and might be holding you back. You have taken steps to reparent your Inner Child to give them what they were missing. And you've looked into what you need in your own personal toolkit in order to set yourself up for success. You are on your way to creating the life that you really want. Now it's time to learn how to affirm that new reality and prepare to chase and achieve your dreams.

Now that you are feeling more confident and beginning to realize your worth, it's time to really let go of the past and focus on yourself. To let go of worrying about what you DO NOT have, and instead be grateful for what you DO have. It's time to begin to appreciate how unique and wonderful you are. Focus on taking care of yourself and releasing anything that holds you back. The final part of letting go of negativity is learning how to forgive. In the coming weeks we will work on releasing any resentment towards those that may have hurt you in the past, even if it was unknowingly. You can't change the past, so let go of that weight. These last four weeks are going to be about bringing it all together. About starting to care more about what your feelings are on the inside rather than what other peoples' feelings are from the outside. Hopefully, by now, you are realizing how wonderful you are, and you're prepared to let go of the past that was holding you back. We will explore concepts that help you ground yourself within your true identity, so that you can live an authentic and fulfilled life. Live consciously–live in the present and take back control of your life. I hope that you are ready to embrace your own beauty and have come to the realization that you truly are a most unique and wonderful being.

week 10: gratitude

"Enjoy the little things in life, for one day you may look back and realize they were the big things."
Robert Bault

GRATITUDE IS AN AMAZING THING. It doesn't take much to learn, but the rewards that it offers are boundless. It has been scientifically proven that practicing gratitude makes us happier and has a healing effect on our psychological, physical and social selves. Studies of the brain have shown that the practice of gratitude can actually rewire our brains and make us happier. You just feel better because you're not focusing on what you don't have. Instead, you're focusing on being thankful for the everyday little things. There are so many people who don't even have that. It really gets you thinking about how privileged you are, even if you don't feel like it. My mom used to say, "There's always someone worse off than you are", and when I learned to practice gratitude that became so much more clear to me. I can be grateful even for something as simple as a pair of socks on a cold day. Not everyone has that. Even on days when everything seems to go wrong, *there is always something to be grateful for.*

Someone once told me that gratitude is directly connected to the law of attraction. In my experience this has been true. I've noticed that once I stopped thinking negatively and started expressing gratitude for even the little things, more good things started coming my way. My business picked up, I was introduced by chance to a wonderful writing coach who helped me finally begin writing my book, and I was feeling better overall. Gratitude magnetizes you for the things you want. When you're grateful for something you haven't yet received as though you already have it, it collapses time and brings it to you faster.

There are two important things that I have adopted through this practice of gratitude. The first is to change the term "I HAVE to" into the term "I GET to". For example, instead of saying "I HAVE to take my grandmother to her doctor's appointment tomorrow so I can't go for lunch with you", say to yourself, "I GET to take my grandmother to her doctor's appointment tomorrow." When you think about how many people do not get the opportunity to do anything with their grandmother, it changes your perspective. The second important thing is to quit thinking in terms of "Why is this happening TO me," and start thinking about "Why is this happening FOR me?" A good example of this is the disastrous relationship that I was so devastated to have lost, but in the end it was the best thing that ever happened to me. It was the beginning of my healing journey and my first step to becoming my authentic self.

Weekly Challenge: Every day when you wake up; write down 3 things that you are grateful for. You might have resistance, you might not feel like doing it; but as an experiment, make sure you do this. The daily exercises will build on this practice and take it deeper. At the end of the week you can check in and see if anything has changed for you.

Weekly Meditation: Week 10–I am Grateful

day 1: "i have to" → "i get to"

TODAY'S AFFIRMATION: *I understand that today is a gift and I am grateful for it.*

FOR AS LONG AS I can remember, I have wanted to have children. I couldn't wait to be a mother. When I was in my early 20's I met a woman who could not have children of her own. We worked across from each other at the mall and sometimes chatted together over lunch. She is one of the sweetest people I have ever met. I remember her telling me that she and her husband had been trying to adopt for a few years. Twice they were told they were going to get a baby and both times the mother changed her mind at the last minute. The second time they were literally on the plane getting ready to take off and travel to the city where the baby was born. I remember thinking how sad it was that these two wonderful people could not conceive the child they so desperately wanted. I even considered being a surrogate for them. Finally, they had an opportunity to adopt a 4 year old child. She told me that she had to write a letter to the mother, telling her why they would be the best choice as adoptive parents. She said to me: "Sandy, it's so hard to write this letter. I'm telling this woman who has to give up her child that I have such a wonderful life! I have a lot of money and a big beautiful house and my husband and I are so happily married. The only thing I need to make my life complete is your child. How do I write that?" In the end, they were able to adopt a beautiful 4 year old girl and made a beautiful, happy family.

I lost touch with this woman eventually, but I still think of her often. This was especially so when I was pregnant and while my children were young. I did not have any trouble getting pregnant, and I thought about her and how much she struggled. I loved being pregnant and I had few difficulties. I had very little morning sickness. If I was having a not so good day I tried to remember that woman and to be grateful for the vomiting or the little foot in my ribs because it meant that I was privileged enough to be able to carry a child. When my daughter was born and I had a newborn and an 18 month old, some days were very rough. But I tried to remember that I was such a lucky woman to have two beautiful children to call my own. This is the difference between "I HAVE to' and I GET to'. Did I change what felt like a million diapers? Yes I did. But I GOT to change those diapers because I was blessed to have given birth to two healthy babies.

Think about what you have to do tomorrow. On the next page, break down your day into all of the chores or steps that you need to take. Write them down starting with the words: 'I GET to…". For example:

- I get to wake up early.
- I get to eat breakfast.
- I get to drive my kids to school.

- I get to drive to work.
- Etc.

Once you've gone through your whole day, read the sentences you wrote. Does it make you feel differently at all about your day?

day 2: dig deeper into gratitude

TODAY'S AFFIRMATION: *I appreciate the good in my life; and more good will come to me.*

EVERY SINGLE DAY there is something to be grateful for, if we choose to look for it. It's definitely not always easy, especially if we are going through a rough period. I've been there… many, many times. Those times when it feels like no matter what you do, you just keep getting kicked in the teeth. Those times when you are painting a smile on your face and telling everyone that everything is fine; but inside your soul is screaming in pain. Maybe you feel like you're there right now and as you're reading this you're thinking, "What the hell is she talking about? My life sucks! What the f**k do I have to be grateful for?" Yeah, I've been there. But I will say it again, *there is always something to be grateful for.* Look for it, find it. You're having a really crappy day and you finally get your coffee break. Sit down, breathe, slowly sip your coffee. Be grateful for this coffee break. If you can do this, if you can recognize and be grateful for the smallest things, you will find things change in your life. You will begin to feel happier, and as your brain changes so will the way you feel about your life.

Your Challenge this week is to write down 3 things every day that you are grateful for. Look at what you wrote for today. Choose one of those three things and write down 3 reasons why you are grateful for that thing.

- Example: "I'm grateful for my kids." "What about my kids am I grateful for?" "I'm grateful for the unconditional love that I get to give and receive. I'm grateful for what they are bringing to this world. I'm grateful that I get to watch them become who they are."
- Do the above for each of the 3 things that you are grateful for today.

day 3: gratitude for what's going right

TODAY'S AFFIRMATION: *I remind myself to enjoy all the good in my life.*

WHEN I WAS a child there was a cartoon called The Flintstones on TV. One of the characters on the show was 'Bad Luck Schleprock'. Poor Schleprock was literally followed by bad luck. A dark rain cloud hung over his head wherever he went and he was always muttering, "Oh woe is me." The Law of Attraction, in simple terms, states that positive thoughts will bring positive results and negative thoughts will bring negative results. When things are going right, a lot of people will tense up, waiting for "the other shoe to drop." I think we have all had those moments when we just expect the worst. This inevitably breaks the momentum of positive events and introduces tension. When you're catching a wave of positive events, it's important to draw from and enjoy those positive emotions as much as possible. This builds and sustains the momentum of the positive emotions and events, and draws more of what you want into your life. Positive thinking can reduce anxiety, stress and tension; as well as having positive effects on your overall health. We need to be aware of our thoughts and be aware that positive thoughts will attract more and more success and happiness into our lives.

Think of something that is going right in your life.

- What are you most excited about right now?

- What are you most afraid of when things seem to be going right?

Make sure to express your gratitude for everything that is going right.

day 4: gratitude for what's going wrong

TODAY'S AFFIRMATION: *I know there is something good in every situation.*

ONE OF THE best days I ever spent with my mom was while she was undergoing chemotherapy. When she started to lose all of her hair, she shaved her head and we went to the wig store. We spent a few hours there while she tried on all different kinds of wigs. Different lengths, different styles, different colors. Some of them made us laugh, some of them looked fabulous. We were having a lot of fun. She laughed so hard when I suggested that she should get two or three different ones so that her husband could feel like he was seeing a different woman every day. My mom was a natural blonde, but one of the wigs she put on was red. It made me do a double take. I looked at her and said, "Holy crap, mom! You look amazing as a redhead!" She ended up buying the red wig. She was really happy that day. It was such a positive, happy moment in such a terrible time. I can't speak for her, but it was almost as if she was grateful for the way that she looked in that red wig. I will never forget how she glowed that day.

Think of a situation that is making you suffer.

- Find the silver lining in the negative. Feel gratitude for the gifts that this situation has given you so far.
- What has it taught you?
- How has it deepened your relationships?
- What have you done (or been able to do) because of this situation that otherwise you wouldn't have done (or been able to do)?

day 5: gratitude for the past

TODAY'S AFFIRMATION: *I recognize that there is a silver lining in every tough experience.*

WHEN I TELL people about my life, they often ask me: "If you could go back to any point in time and change anything, would you?" I often joke about how my life could be one of those made for TV movies: a broken home, a deadbeat alcoholic dad, a teen marriage, an abusive husband, a rare autoimmune disease…and so much more. One day I will tell the whole story. But would I change anything? Absolutely not. All of the pain made me the person that I am today, and I love this person. Everyone has or will experience something traumatic in their lifetime: death of a family member or close friend, bad relationships, illness, or abuse. Even just moving to a different location can be traumatic. Everything that you have been through has brought you to this moment in time. Every experience, every heartbreak, every victory has made you who you are, and you are amazing!

Sandy Lynn

Reflect on everything, positive and negative, that has brought you to where you are today. Show yourself some gratitude. Write a thank you note to yourself for getting you to this point.

day 6 : what went right?

TODAY'S AFFIRMATION: *I appreciate the simple pleasures that make my day beautiful.*

I HAVE BEEN on my healing journey for a while now; but sometimes I still need reminders to be present and grateful. This happens when things are going right and when things are going wrong. I may have had a fantastic week in which so many positive things happened that I forget to just take a minute to be thankful. Or, it's a crazy, horrible week and I don't feel thankful at all. Either way, it's important to get into the habit of being present and being aware of even the little things. For example, at the dinner table instead of asking your spouse "How was your day?" or asking your kids: "What did you do at school today?" ask instead: "What went right today?"

Ask yourself: "What went right this week?" How many things can you think of that went right? Write down anything you can think of. Remember, they don't have to be huge, epic things. It can be as simple as 'the line at the drive through was really short and I was able to get my favorite coffee before work.'

day 7: free write

TODAY'S AFFIRMATION: *I choose to see the light in my life.*

TODAY IS A 'FREE WRITE'. Write about any feelings you had while completing this week's exercises. Were there any surprises? What did you learn about yourself? How did you do with this week's Challenge? Feel free to write about anything and everything that comes into your head. Get it out, free your mind, put it on the paper.

Sandy Lynn

Complete this statement: I AM

week 11: forgiveness

"The weak can never forgive. Forgiveness is the attribute of the strong."
Mahatma Ghandi

THERE SEEMS to be two camps when it comes to forgiveness. For some there is the belief that you must forgive in order to heal; that it is impossible to get past any kind of trauma unless you can forgive the one who wronged you. On the other side of that is the thought that forgiveness does nothing for you, it just makes the wrongdoer feel better. Part of the problem is that there are so many common misconceptions about what forgiveness actually means and involves. If you forgive someone it's not because you are the bigger or better person. It's not you saying that what they did was okay and that you can get past it. Forgiveness is actually you recognizing their humanity and bringing both of you onto the same level. When you truly forgive someone you stop seeing them as guilty and you are able to see them with compassion. Forgiveness is the act of setting YOURSELF free.

Not setting the other person free. It doesn't matter what they did or why they did it. You are making an agreement with yourself to no longer let what they did to you affect your life path.

Another issue behind forgiveness is the depth and the complexity of the emotions behind it. More often than not, the biggest reason that we cannot forgive someone is because we are so angry about what they did. Brene Brown, in her book "Atlas of the Heart" talks about how anger is a secondary emotion, not a primary emotion. This means that anger is like a check engine light. It tells you that something is wrong, but doesn't tell you what. Anger happens when you have unacknowledged and unexpressed emotion. Many things can be at the root of anger: frustration, sadness, overwhelm, etc. Understanding the source of your own anger allows you to practice compassion and love for yourself, and, in turn, for the one who did you wrong.

Forgiveness can also allow us to maintain relationships with close friends or family members who we feel have wronged us but from whom we feel that we cannot just simply walk away. We connect with others on the level of our pain or on the level of our spirit. You build relationships with others through your dysfunction or through your strengths. As you release your limiting beliefs, you also permanently alter the relationships that were built on dysfunction. These relationships will have to adjust to the new you or they will fall away. If you are able to understand the source of your anger with this person, you may be able to see them in a different light. You may be able to move forward and create a new relationship based on your mutual strengths rather than your mutual pain. Sometimes people are not able to do that, and you may have to choose to change the essence of that relationship in order to do what is best for you. When you are prepared to say goodbye to anything that is not serving your highest good, you will feel the changes in your life: physically, emotionally and spiritually.

Sometimes the person that we have to forgive is ourselves. This is one of the hardest things to realize; and one of the hardest things to do. In almost any given situation, even if someone else has done us wrong, our human make up causes us to feel guilt for some part of it. This is another area where the 'Shoulda Coulda Wouldas' tend to pop up. The abused woman tells herself that if she hadn't talked back to her partner she wouldn't have been hit. The victim of a mugging blames themselves afterwards for not fighting back. Our society has an awful tendency to blame the victim, and the victims then blame themselves. Part of our personal healing has to be letting go of that guilt and forgiving ourselves. If we have done something wrong to someone else, that guilt may eat away at us for years and years. I remember many sleepless nights where I relived the tiniest transgression from 30 years in the past. The pain and guilt that I carried from other incidents, the low self esteem and lack of self compassion that I carried made it difficult for me to realize that, in the end, I am only human and I will make mistakes. I had to learn how to show the same compassion that I had shown others to myself.

Let's talk about *unforgiveness* for a minute. Imagine that someone took a very large knife and stabbed you in the stomach. You went to the hospital for treatment and the wound healed; but emotionally you are still very hurt and angry. Your hurt and your anger leads you to dwell on this story of being stabbed, and every time you tell the story of being stabbed you grab a large knife and stab yourself in the same place over and over so that you can remind yourself how much this person hurt you. Ultimately, you are acting and speaking out of your own anger about what happened. The other person stabbed you only once, but you refuse to let go of the story. You refuse to let go of what they did. The initial action created a storyline that you have a hard time letting go of. Essentially, you are letting the other person become the author of YOUR story. It's up to you to take back control by letting go and forgiving. Tell your own damn story!

Weekly Challenge: In Part 3 Week 1 we learned about Ho'Oponopono and we practiced it on your Inner Child. This week I would like you to go back and review the principles of Ho'Oponopono and utilize this practice on your adult self. Every day this week take some time to say these phrases to yourself, with whatever additions you feel that you need:

- **"I love you"** (I love you so much)
- **"I'm sorry,"** (I'm sorry for being hard on you, for all of your pain, etc.)
- **"Please forgive me,"** (for not always being there for you, etc.)
- **"Thank you,"** (for being so strong, for not giving up on me, etc)

Weekly Meditation: Week 11–Forgiving Yourself

day 1: what are you struggling to forgive?

TODAY'S AFFIRMATION: *As I let go I feel myself blooming in all areas of my life.*

I HAVE WORKED HARD at forgiveness, both for those that I felt did me wrong and for myself. It has not been an easy road. Some people I talked to in person and we worked out the issue. In other cases a face to face talk was not a possibility so I wrote about it in my journal. I wrote down what I would say to that person if I had the opportunity. With myself I have used a combination of modalities like Ho'Oponopono, meditation, Inner Child journaling and Breathwork.

I would like to tell you that I have worked through everything and forgiven everyone and that my life is beautiful all the time, but that would not be the truth and it is not realistic. I am only human, and there are people in my life that I had to work very hard to forgive. It took me a lot of years to finally forgive my father for abandoning our family. Between my anger and my father's shame for his behavior we wasted a lot of time. My father passed away just over a year ago and I am so glad that we were able to mend our relationship before he passed.

What is a situation or person you have a hard time forgiving? Do you think you will ever forgive?

day 2: the reason behind your unforgiveness

TODAY'S AFFIRMATION: *My heart is open to forgiveness and compassion.*

ONE OF THE reasons it took me so long to forgive my father is because I never really acknowledged my feelings about what he had done. It was so confusing to love a person so much and to want their approval so badly, yet at the same time be so angry with him. So angry that my anger consumed me. How dare he treat me like that! *Unforgiveness* becomes its own entity. It grows. If you keep feeding it with your anger, it becomes a situation where every little thing the other person does angers you even further, and it becomes a bigger thing. You will get to a point where you are looking for things that they are doing wrong to you. You will focus on their actions and words and immediately interpret them as a means to wrong you, even if they had nothing to do with you. You will keep bringing forward things that happened 30 years ago, telling yourself: "Remember that time they did this too?"

Often it's hard to forgive, because we're not acknowledging

what we're actually feeling. If we go back to Brene Brown's book and think about the idea of anger as a secondary emotion, the question then becomes: "What is behind the anger? What am I actually feeling when it comes to this person?" When I answer this question, it is important to note that these are my feelings, from my perspective. Whether right or wrong, I take ownership of these feelings.

Think back to the situation you wrote about yesterday. Why are you having a hard time forgiving? What are you angry about?

day 3: recognizing what's underneath the anger

TODAY'S AFFIRMATION: *I forgive for my own sake.*

AS I ACKNOWLEDGED MY ANGER, I had to start thinking about what was underneath all of it. I had to let myself admit what my true feelings were about the whole situation. And I must emphasize here that these are ***my feelings*** **from** ***my perspective. From my point of view*** as a child, nothing that I did was ever good enough. My dad left me, my mom loved my sister more than me, I didn't get along with my stepfather. I felt like I had nobody in my corner. As I got older I let these feelings dictate my worth and how I felt about myself. I stayed in relationships where I was mistreated. I allowed people to take advantage of me. I had no boundaries. As I worked through my emotions, I realized that part of the problem was that I had been blaming myself for his actions. Why wasn't I good enough for him to want to stay with us? Or at least come and visit me? I had been robbed of the father/daughter relationship I had always dreamed of.

These inner feelings of being abandoned had caused such a

deep rooted pain that it affected every area of my life. Underneath all of the anger, my inner child was spiralling. She had been looking her entire life for that feeling of unconditional love. The problem was that her need for acceptance was so strong that she became a chameleon, changing herself to suit the needs of all of the other people in her life. When the adult me started learning to love herself the way she was, my inner child was able to relax and release all of the heavy emotions she had been carrying.

Sometimes our parents/caregivers make mistakes when raising us. Is your Inner Child still angry about the actions of the adults in his/her childhood? What are some of these actions? Think about the emotions hidden under your anger. How can you help your Inner Child to move on from this?

day 4: taking responsibility

TODAY'S AFFIRMATION: *I am forgiving myself for mistakes in my past.*

PART OF RECOGNIZING your emotions is to recognize your responsibility, not necessarily during the events but afterward. As a child I did not have a lot of control over what was happening in my life, but as an adult I am responsible for the choices I make. I never told my father how I felt about what he had done. I never held him responsible when he floated in and out of my life. I just let him, and was grateful for the time I did get to spend with him. So many people wondered why I even spoke to him anymore. To be honest, I wasn't even sure myself. I just kept forgiving him.

When I became a parent myself I started to think differently. I knew that there was no way in hell that anybody or anything would keep me from my children. So, how could my father let alcohol or women or shame get in the way of him coming to see me and my sister. How could I allow him to do the same thing to my children? There was no way that I was going to let him float in and out of their lives as well. That's when I became very angry, and when he didn't show up to see my children when he said he was going to, I just exploded! The pain, the feelings of abandonment, the unspoken words; they all came out in one big volcanic eruption. I really let him have it! I told him that if he wanted to be a part of my children's life he needed to be there, and if he didn't plan on doing that then he just shouldn't bother. After that we didn't speak for many years. Between my anger and my father's shame, many years were wasted. Thankfully, through my healing process I was able to get past my anger, take responsibility for my part, and reach out to him. During our time of estrangement my father had also met a woman who was helping him to accept responsibility for his actions and move forward. We were able to mend our relationship and I spent many wonderful days with him and his family. He passed away last year and I miss him every single day.

I am an adult now and I have a voice. I am allowed to speak my mind and voice my opinion. That is my responsibility. Staying silent in one's anger only aggravates the situation. When you take responsibility for your part, you won't have to take responsibility for theirs. You will be able to stop blaming both them and yourself.

When you look closely at the situation or at the person that you have not forgiven, can you see anything that you should take responsibility for? What can you take responsibility for, and forgive yourself for, so that you can move forward in trying to forgive them?

day 5 : the reasons behind their behavior

TODAY'S AFFIRMATION: *I release anger and embrace peace.*

EVERYTHING HAPPENS FOR A REASON, and there is a reason behind every action. We've all heard the saying, 'Hurt people hurt people'. If I apply this to my situation, no one was *intentionally* trying to hurt me. My mother was 17 years old, pregnant and married to a man who was an alcoholic and unfaithful. Her father wasn't the most affectionate man from what I remember. My father was just a kid himself. I don't know a lot about his childhood but I do know that his father wasn't around a lot when he was a child because of his work. He was the youngest of four and I have been told that he was quite spoiled by my grandmother. In her eyes he could do no wrong. Hard to suddenly be responsible for a wife and child when you've never really been held responsible for anything in your life. My stepfather was strict and authoritarian because that's the way he was raised. He didn't know anything else. He was also younger than my mother and stepped into a situation where suddenly he was expected to be a father to two young girls. They were all learning on the job. We all do the best we can with the tools that we have.

Think about your situation. Did the person who hurt you do it on purpose? What might be the reasons behind their actions? Choose the person or situation you've been wanting to release, and go through Ho'Oponopono. (I love you, I'm sorry, Please forgive me, Thank you.) Also, it's okay if, like me, you are still working towards total forgiveness. If you can't say 'I love you' say 'I send you love'. If you can't forgive completely, think of something that you can forgive. And if you can't say it out loud, at least start by writing it down.

day 6: you are not your mistakes (forgiving yourself)

TODAY'S AFFIRMATION: *I forgive myself for the mistakes of my past.*

WHEN YOU CAN RECOGNIZE and accept your true feelings about a situation, then you are able to step back from them. You stop letting them rule your life and become your identity. You are then able to separate your identity from your mistakes. Release them. Release yourself from their weight and apply love and compassion. As I go through this process I can feel myself coming closer to forgiveness of myself and others, because I am not letting these feelings dictate how I feel about myself and how I lead my life. I realize that the story that I have been telling is getting old and monotonous and I am ready to write a new one.

ATONEMENT LETTER – Are there any past events in your life that you look back on with regret for your actions or words? How do you deal with this regret? Write a forgiveness letter to yourself. Think about what you might say to someone else that you need to forgive and apply these same words and phrases to yourself.

day 7: free write

TODAY'S AFFIRMATION: *I forgive myself and others, releasing all past hurts.*

TODAY IS A 'FREE WRITE'. Write about any feelings you had while completing this week's exercises. Were there any surprises? What did you learn about yourself? How did you do with this week's Challenge? Feel free to write about anything and everything that comes into your head. Get it out, free your mind, put it on the paper.

Sandy Lynn

Complete this statement: I AM

week 12: self care

"To love oneself is the beginning of a lifelong romance."
Oscar Wilde

A HUGE PART of learning to love yourself is making sure that you take the time for self care. Now I can hear a lot of you saying, "But I do that. I go to my yoga class every week." Or, "I get my nails done every month." Or, "I take a walk every night with my dog." But true self care isn't necessarily an action like getting a massage or taking a long, hot bath. It can be anything you do to take care of yourself: drinking water, resting when you're tired, reading a book, asking for help, allowing yourself to feel your emotions without judgment. The most important thing is that you take some time to understand *your* needs. Everybody is different and relaxes in different ways. For example, something I find really relaxing is going out to my garage and sanding down old wood furniture to refinish it. For someone else, that's a chore. For me, it's part of my self care.

I am kind of a handy person. I like woodworking, sewing and

crocheting. I'm always making something. My daughter suggested once that I start an online store to sell all of the little things I make instead of just giving them away. I said, "No, because if people start ordering things then I'll have to do it. Then it's not relaxing anymore." True self care is giving your body and mind what they need: physically, mentally, emotionally and spiritually. True self care involves caring for your whole self on an ongoing basis. If we can practice self care in this way, it not only reduces stress and allows us to feel better in the short term; but in the long term it can reduce feelings of burnout, help us manage chronic conditions and improve our quality of life overall. This means that self care is not a luxury, it's essential to our overall well-being. So, why is it then, that so many of us neglect this responsibility?

My children's father was a workaholic. He worked 12 - 18 hour days. He worked weekends. His focus was always preparing for retirement. He lived to work to retire. If the kids commented on how he was never home he would say things like, "The more I work the more money we have to do things like going to Disneyland." One of the reasons that he said he wanted to take the job overseas was because it paid such great money, so even though he would be gone for 6 weeks at a time he could probably retire early and spend more time at home. The kids are adults now, and we never took them to Disneyland. And that hard-working man passed away at the age of 57, so he never made it to retirement. Not long after he passed, my son came to me to tell me about his new job. He had worked so hard in school to complete his engineering degree, but unfortunately he graduated during the COVID pandemic and had difficulty obtaining employment in his field. For the longest time he beat himself up about that. But when he got this specific position he said, "Mom, it's not an engineering job, but it's a really good job. And I'll be home every night and every weekend with my family." I was so proud of him at that moment.

Western society devalues self care. The whole culture does. We do that with statements like, "work hard, play hard." "No pain, no gain." We have long work days that don't allow for midday resting. We often pass judgment when someone does take the time to take care of themselves. This is one of the reasons why South Korean visual artist Woopsyang created the Space Out Competition, which centers around the art of doing nothing. The goal of the competition is to see who can maintain the lowest heart rate. Woopsyang said she came up with the idea when she began to notice that so many people in our society did not take the time for much needed rest. We push ourselves to burn out because we have developed the crazy idea that if we are not keeping busy we are wasting time, so she created a competition that brings a group of people together with the *intention* of doing nothing and being the best at it. Since the first event was held in Seoul in 2014, it is now being held in other international cities like Beijing, Rotterdam, and Taipei.

A huge side effect of not prioritizing self care in western culture is anxiety. Almost every single person that I know has had a period in their life where they dealt with severe anxiety. I feel that a lot of anxiety comes from people being overwhelmed and not having good self-care tools. They're not releasing all this excess emotion, whether it's stress or fear or guilt or whatever it is. For my daughter, part of her self care routine is working out at the gym on a daily basis. When she misses too many days in a row at the gym, her anxiety goes way up because she hasn't had an opportunity to really release. Some people release through drawing or knitting. Everyone develops their own tools. If you don't allow yourself the space and the time to release, you're not letting go of the negative emotions that are building up inside you. We are even seeing a rise in the amount of young children who suffer from anxiety. They're surrounded by very loud negative voices everywhere, and we're not teaching them how to release the negativity through self-care. What are you teaching your children when you don't take care of yourself? You're teaching them to become adults who put other people's needs ahead of their own to their own detriment. On the other hand, when you demonstrate taking care of yourself and practicing self care, you teach them to fill up their own energy reserves before they give to others. It's become almost an epidemic, and a lot of it is because people are not taking care of themselves. Their bodies and souls are screaming "Take care of me!"

So, this week we are going to work on your self care habits, and I would like you to stop thinking of self care as selfish. I want you to know that it can feel like work at first. You're trying to create this whole new habit. For some of you, you might have to make a schedule to make sure that you are getting your daily self care. You also might feel guilty about taking the time to yourself. DON'T! And when life gets busy, you are going to want to cut your self care because it feels frivolous and indulgent. IT'S NOT! There's nothing more selfless than taking care of yourself, because if you're depleted, you have nothing to give. Self care is also honoring what you want to do in the world. Being honest about your passions, your interests, and what brings you joy and fulfillment. I wrote a few days back about 'wants' and 'needs'. Remember, sometimes a want is actually a need, needed in order to feed your soul.

Weekly Challenge: Take a 2 minute self appreciation break every day. Slow down, take a breath and acknowledge everything you like about yourself. What is it about yourself that you find appealing? Write these things in your journal. If you're having a bad day, stop what you're doing and take this break…and see how the day changes.

Weekly Meditation: Week 12–I am Worthy, I am Loved, I am Enough

day 1: what do you do for self care?

TODAY'S AFFIRMATION: *I will be kind to myself today.*

FROM A VERY YOUNG age I had dreams of becoming a performer. I wanted to sing and dance and be famous. I wished that I could take lessons, but my single mother worked hard to barely make ends meet. There was no way she could afford lessons of any kind. I was taught as a child that the world was an unfair place, and that, essentially, we are here to work hard in order to survive until we die. I used to look up to my father for following his dreams of being in a band, but at the same time I was aware that he was looked down upon for that very same thing. My mom busted her ass to keep us fed, and I never saw her do anything for herself. It was ingrained in me that self care was a frivolous waste of time. I lived my whole life this way. As I started moving into my 40's, I started to question this idea. I lived with a man who worked very hard, and I loved and admired him for it for many years. But I started to question what it was all for. There had to be more to life than working at your job all day and then working at home all evening and then going to bed, only to get up and do it all again the next day. Working hard and saving for tomorrow now seemed a waste of time to me, because tomorrow never really came.

Think about your self care routine:

- What does self care mean to you?

- How often do you engage in self care activities?

- What specifically do you do as part of your daily self care?

- How do you feel when you do these things? (peaceful? guilty? selfish? deserving?)

day 2: what do you want/need?

TODAY'S AFFIRMATION: *I listen to my thoughts and feelings.*

SELF CARE INVOLVES TAKING care of your own wants and needs so you can show up fully. Most people don't know what their needs are because they don't even ask the question, "What do I want? What do I need?". It took me a long time to figure out exactly what would feed my soul. A lot of it was trial and error. I do know that I need to have it built right into my daily routine or I will neglect it and let it fall by the wayside. I also think that the needs that a person has for their personal self care will change at different times throughout their lives. Right now, for me, it involves doing all of the things that I have always wanted to do. I am building my self esteem and self confidence. When I can do that, I feel better. I feel good about myself. When I feel good about myself I tend to stick more to my healthy eating habits and exercise routines. It's important to remember that self care isn't just physical, but also emotional and spiritual. Everything is connected.

Think about what you want and need in these areas of your life. Remember that a want can also be a need:

- Physically
    - How much rest do you need?

- What foods?

- How much exercise? What kind of exercise?

- Fun stuff (nails done, hair done, etc.

- Anything else you can think of?

- Emotionally/Mentally
    - Relationships / Family

- Career

- Love life

- Fun stuff (concerts, classes, reading, etc)

- Anything else?

- Spiritual
    - What do you need for your own personal fulfillment?

- Being out in nature.

I Am...

- What needs are being met? What needs are NOT being met?

day 3: what needs can you address?

TODAY'S AFFIRMATION: *I make sure that all of my needs are being met.*

OFTEN, when you want to lose weight, you will follow a diet plan, use certain recipes, and do your meal prep ahead of time. These are things that are suggested to help us be successful in losing weight. You could actually apply this concept to your whole life. If you are planning on building any kind of self care routine, you need to schedule it right into your day. This will help keep you on track and help you to be successful, until it becomes second nature. I have already mentioned that I need a schedule, and if I don't follow it, it doesn't take long for me to 'fall off the wagon'. For example, I have a schedule posted on my wall, and every morning I have scheduled time for meditation and breathwork. And if you think time might be an issue, think about the amount of time you spend scrolling online or watching tv. Could you possibly find time for a 30 minute soak in a tub or 15 minutes of meditation? Actually, don't even answer that question. Just MAKE TIME!

Think about the needs you wrote down yesterday.

- What's doable? What can I accomplish?

- How do you prioritize these?

- How can you build these into your daily routine?

day 4: find what works for you/creating peace of mind

TODAY'S AFFIRMATION: *I will pursue my passions with patience, focus and strength.*

A VERY IMPORTANT part of self care is calming your mind. Many of us find this very difficult to do. We are all unique beings, and because of that, we all need different tools in our toolkit. What works for you may not work for me, and vice versa. I tried many different modalities to start my healing: yoga, body talk, meditation. I enjoyed them all and they all worked for me to some extent; but it wasn't until I started doing breathwork that the spark was ignited. That particular form of self care started a chain reaction in my brain. This is when I realized how important it was for me to be a little bit selfish. So many things have happened since then, including the decision to finally write this book, and I'm not looking back.

You need to find what works for you. It might be physical, like working out at the gym. It could be something creative like painting or drawing. Maybe meditation will be your thing. Or a combination of things, like Meditative Drawing. I've talked before about creating space for yourself and decluttering. Is that something that you need to do? Take a look around you, take a look inside you. Think about what might work for you.

Do you make a point of calming your mind for at least a short time every day?

- Do you find this difficult? Why?

- Have you tried different modalities (meditation, yoga, working out)?

- What works for you and what doesn't?

- Research some different techniques and give them a try.

day 5: the importance of rest

TODAY'S AFFIRMATION: *I am calm and peaceful when I take good care of myself.*

WE DEFINITELY TEND to underestimate the importance of quality sleep and rest. Yes, physically our bodies need rest: a good night's sleep, a nap, or maybe even some yoga and stretching. But we need rest in different areas as well. One of the things I often say after a long day of teaching or dealing with stress is, "My brain is tired." This means I just need to empty it out and give it a little rest. Mental rest is just as important as physical rest. Just sitting in silence for a few minutes can make all of the difference. Emotionally, if we are bottling up a lot of negative feelings it can be exhausting. We need to achieve emotional rest through releasing those emotions by processing them and letting them go. I have been emotionally exhausted for most of my life. It is just in the last few years that I have learned to let go.

As long as I can remember I have always struggled with sleep, especially just the act of falling asleep. To this day, I know that I need to do some more work in that area. I have sleep apnea, so I use a CPAP machine. I have recently found out that I have iron deficiency anemia, so that has helped me understand why I feel so tired all of the time. But I also know that my sleep routines and patterns are terrible, and these are things that are under my control. I just have not made them enough of a priority. One of my biggest issues is that since my mom passed away, I have not been able to fall asleep without the television on. Unfortunately, that really affects my sleep quality. The worst part about it is, I know what I need to do, and I try, but I keep slipping back into the bad habits. The main thing is that I keep trying. I'm getting better. I look forward to the day when I break that habit completely.

It is so important to actually set yourself up for a peaceful sleep. Some suggestions might be:

- Early supper so that you can digest everything before you lay down.
- Reduce alcohol consumption before sleep (it over stimulates the liver and causes restlessness)
- Cool foot bath
- Uncluttered, clean sleep space
- Consider a weighted blanket
- Self massage-lower back, feet, ears, head, feet
- Unplug for at least an hour before sleep
- Dim the lights / play soft music or white noise
- Journaling, meditation etc. (whatever works for you)
    - What went right today?
    - What's one thing about today that you're grateful for?
- Head South feet North

Think about your rest patterns:

- What kinds of things do you do to give yourself some rest physically, mentally and emotionally?

- How are your sleep patterns?

- Do you have an 'end of the day' routine? Do you feel like you need one?

- What kind of a sleep routine can you start for yourself?

day 6: making self care a part of your routine

TODAY'S AFFIRMATION: *Taking care of myself makes me healthy and happy.*

IF YOU'RE anything like me, habits are difficult for you, both breaking the bad ones and starting a new good one. I have to start off very disciplined and rigid until I form the actual habit, and then it becomes second nature to me and I don't know how I ever did things differently. For example, when I decided that I wanted to start meditating I couldn't just say, "I'm going to try meditating every day for 15 minutes." I had to actually schedule it into my day; every day at 8 p.m., while I was getting ready for bed, I would meditate for 15 minutes. Another thing that worked well for me was to schedule workout time first thing in the morning; and then time for journaling and meditation as part of my 'end of the day' routine. Worried about fitting everything in? Sometimes it's just a matter of waking up 15 minutes earlier in the morning, or shutting the screens off half an hour earlier in the evening. Sitting alone for 10 minutes on your lunch break to clear your mind. If you make a schedule you will see how easy it is to fit everything in. It's also important to remember not to be too hard on yourself if you slip; just get back at it and keep on trying.

Make yourself a daily schedule that includes self care, whatever that may look like for you. Once you've got it laid out, make a really nice copy, decorate it however you would like, and post it on your bedroom wall so that you see it every morning.

day 7: free write

TODAY'S AFFIRMATION: *I am doing a fabulous job being me.*

TODAY IS A 'FREE WRITE'. Write about any feelings you had while completing this week's exercises. Were there any surprises? What did you learn about yourself? How did you do with this week's Challenge? Feel free to write about anything and everything that comes into your head. Get it out, free your mind, put it on the paper.

Sandy Lynn

Complete the following statement: I AM

week 13: affirm a new reality

> "And when you're alone, there's a very good chance
> you'll meet things that scare you right out of your pants.
> There are some, down the road between hither and yon,
> that can scare you so much you won't want to go on.
> But on you will go though the weather be foul.
> On you will go though your enemies prowl.
> On you will go though the Hakken-Kraks howl...
> On and on you will hike. And I know you'll hike far
> and face up to your problems whatever they are.
> And will you succeed? Yes! You will, indeed!
> (98 and ¾ percent guaranteed.) ...
> Kid, you'll move mountains!"
> Dr. Seuss, Oh, the Places You'll Go!

AS I HAVE GONE through my own journey I have watched myself become more and more my authentic self. This is the Inner Child that was trapped. She was stuck in the lack mentality that had been passed down through my family from generation to generation. I am stepping away from the version of me that had the same dreams year after year but always found an excuse not to follow through. There was always a reason: not enough time, not enough money, the thought that I wasn't ready, fear. The biggest excuse of course was that I spent too much time listening to other people tell me what I was capable of, what I was meant for; allowing others to judge my dreams. Now, when I want to do something, I do it. I'm taking the dance classes. I'm taking the theater classes. I'm taking the time to write the book, if that is what my soul needs to do. That is a part of who I am, and I don't give a damn what anybody else thinks.

I hope that when you look in the mirror now, you see a much more confident version of you; the you that loves who you are. Think about how you are showing up in the world differently now than you were when you first started reading this book. Now is the time for you to begin envisioning your perfect life! Put more thought into what your goals, hobbies and passions are. Go after them! Make plans and follow through with them. Not sure exactly what you want to do? That's okay. Neither was I. I knew I was meant to do something. I knew there was something that my soul was yearning for. I just didn't know what it was. I had to try new things and step out of my comfort zone to find out. Get inspired by reading, listening to podcasts, trying things you've never done but had always been curious about. Get off social media and out of the habit of comparing yourself and your life to others.

Now it's time to see and live your dream as if it's already happened. You are ready to love yourself, and in turn you will spread love and kindness to others. In the Introduction, we talked a bit about Affirmations, and you have been using these on a daily basis in order to bring forward the power of positive thought. It's time for you to create affirmations of your own, specific to your life and your dreams. You have to believe that you can use the power of your mind to create your reality. If the past and future don't exist, and if you're constantly creating your reality with your mind, then why not use your mind to create and live a reality you actually want to experience? When you change your thoughts in the moment, you change your reality, and as a result your future. Your thoughts in the moment determine who you are right now and so, they determine the reality you'll live in the future.

We have come to the final week of our journey. You are 7 days away from the finish line! This week we are going to focus on celebrating and being grateful for the beautiful individual that you are! How are we going to keep this momentum going so that you continue to love yourself more and more, and create the life that you've always wanted to have? Over the next 7 days we will take a look at how far you've come, and create a vision of where you want to go. Let's shake off the last bits of that old personality that does not match the next version of yourself. It's important to note here that I don't mean you need to change the core of your being. What's really happening is that you've taken off the protective mask that you've been wearing for so long, and you're finally becoming the person that you were always meant to be.

Weekly Challenge: This week your challenge is to create a Vision Board. A Vision Board is basically a creative way to visualize your future goals. It's a collage of pictures, words and phrases that inspire you to stay on track. Some people create Vision Boards every year to set their intentions for the year. Check out these websites if you need some inspiration:

- https://www.scienceofpeople.com/how-to-make-a-vision-board/
  - https://www.psychologytoday.com/us/blog/click-here-happiness/202103/what-is-vision-board-and-why-make-one

Weekly Meditation: Week 13–I Am, I Can, I Will

day 1: changing

TODAY'S AFFIRMATION: *I am worthy of beautiful endings and exciting beginnings.*

ONE OF THE most exciting things for me about going through this whole healing process is being able to recognize and stop old behaviors. Shortly after I got out of that terrible narcissistic relationship, I met a wonderful man. He was kind, loving and affectionate. We had so much in common and enjoyed each other's company. I started to think that maybe I had finally met my person. I was very honest with him about my past, and my wants and needs. I know that my old pattern had been to immediately jump fully into a relationship, ignoring any red flags, because I wanted things to work so badly, and because I wanted to have 'someone' and I didn't like being alone. I told him that I wanted to take it very slowly. He agreed.

I'm not going to go into too much detail, but before too long I started to see that he was moving a lot faster than I was comfortable with. I became torn between knowing that things were moving too fast, and not wanting to give up on having this wonderful person in my life. I realized that I was falling back into my old patterns of not voicing what I was feeling. So I started to communicate more. The problem was that, the more I voiced my feelings, the more we began to argue. I knew that I had to break it off, but the thought of hurting someone hurt me just as much. It was also hard because there was so much about this person that I liked very much, but I was no longer the person who would change her personality and put aside her wants and needs to make someone else happy. So we broke up. He made the comment that maybe I was scared to be in a relationship. I thought about it for a minute and my response was, "I'm not afraid to be in a relationship. I'm afraid to stay in a relationship that I'm not happy in, just for the sake of being in a relationship."

What are some of the behaviors that you will no longer tolerate from yourself? From others?

day 2: what lights you up?

TODAY'S AFFIRMATION: *I am worthy because I say so, my worth is in my hands.*

AS I AM BECOMING my authentic self, I am finding out more and more about what truly feeds my soul. I have different ideas about what is important in life. Not everybody agrees with my new way of thinking but that's okay, they don't have to. One of the amazing things that has happened is that as I take steps forward the opportunities keep coming. The Breathwork led me to Jay Bradley, Jay and the Breathwork helped build my self confidence and rewire my brain. After that I had the courage to take the dance classes, which has now led to theater classes. I have started to talk to people about things I've always kept hidden. The people that I am meeting are connecting me with other people, who I am learning from. I was recently connected with someone who does Human Design readings; and I discovered that I am a Projector. This explains so much to me about why I am the way I am. As a very brief explanation, Human Design is a blend of ancient and modern science that assists an individual to discover their life purposes and energy type. Being a Projector means that I am able to tap into the energy of others and assist them to navigate through a difficult situation, but it also means that I sometimes get overloaded with energy and need time to myself to rest and recharge. (For those of you not familiar with Human Design, check it out if you get a chance). I have also developed the confidence in myself to freely say out loud to others that I am an energy healer and a writer. I hope that you too have built up the courage to be who you want to be and speak your truth.

If you could share one secret about yourself with others, with no repercussions, what would it be? Is there anything stopping you from telling your story?

day 3: chasing your dreams

TODAY'S AFFIRMATION: *I have the freedom and power to create the life I desire.*

I AM LIVING my dream at this moment. As I am writing these words, I am living one of my dreams. As you are reading these words and going through the last week of your journey, keep in mind that as I was writing them I was coming to the last week of living my dream. My book is almost finished, and I cannot even begin to find the words to describe this feeling. The fact that I have actually accomplished this is almost surreal to me. It has taken a lot of work, and I'm not just talking about the writing itself. It's the inner work that was the hardest and took the longest. I know it might sound cliche, but I am living proof that you can overcome your past, you can battle the demons and win! I cannot wait until each and every one of you go out and achieve your dream and feel this feeling.

- What is a dream you never pursued?

- What can you do to make this a reality?

- Break it down into smaller goals. Write them down. Are these smaller goals attainable?

Think about it: What if everything you need is already here?

day 4: recognizing how far you've come

TODAY'S AFFIRMATION: *I am thankful that with each experience I become a better version of myself.*

IT'S SO important to give yourself credit for all of your accomplishments. Even the baby steps. Even when you feel that you're stuck. Especially when you're feeling stuck. You need a reminder of your inner power and what you can actually do. I do that often by rereading my journal or my blog entries just to remind myself of the changes in my thinking. Today we are going back to the beginning so that you can see how far you have come. Let's go back to the flower exercise that you did the first week of this journal.

The 'Feel Wheel' diagram on the next page has 12 sections. Each section represents either a positive or negative feeling or viewpoint that you may have about yourself.

- Starting in the center of the wheel, color each section

so that it represents how often or how strongly you have these feelings.
- Use any color(s) you like for the positive feelings, and use black for the negative feelings.
- What does your 'Feel Wheel' look like? How colorful is it? How does this make you feel?

When you have completed the Feel Wheel, go back to PART 1 Week 1 and compare it to the exercise you completed 13 weeks ago.

- What has changed?
- How are you feeling now?

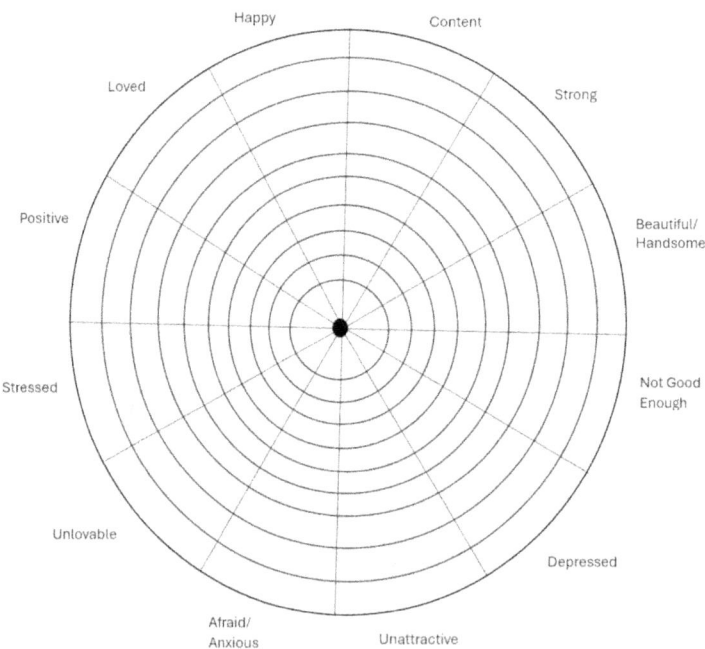

I Am...

day 5: mirror mirror, part 2

TODAY'S AFFIRMATION: *I am grateful for the small steps I take towards loving myself more and more each day.*

TODAY WE ARE GOING BACK AGAIN to an exercise we did in Week 1. This time, before you complete the exercise, do the Weekly Meditation and take some time to show gratitude for yourself and the progress that you've made. Think about all of the steps you have made and the things that you have discovered about yourself. Practice some Ho'Oponopono and show some love to your Inner Child, he or she has worked so hard right along with you. When you feel ready, complete the exercise below.

Undress down to your underwear, or more if you feel comfortable doing so. Now stand in front of the mirror and spend at least 5 minutes looking at yourself. See your entire body from head to toe. Make a mental note of how you feel about everything you see.

This time, before you finish, look deep inside and find your

Inner Child. See him/her. Give him/her, and yourself, big **HUGS.** Honor the entire process you've been through.

Light your favorite candle. Write about everything you felt while you were looking in the mirror. Do you feel any differently than you did in Week 1? If you are still carrying any negative thoughts (and don't beat yourself up if you are) write them down on a separate piece of paper. Then fold this piece of paper in half, facing away from you. Fold it once or twice more, always facing away from you. Now burn it and blow the ashes away (or rinse them down the sink with water). You can also tear it into tiny pieces and let it go in the trash. While you are 'getting rid of' these negative statements, say TODAY'S AFFIRMATION out loud as many times as you need to.

day 6: effective personal affirmations

TODAY'S AFFIRMATION: *Write Your Own*

THROUGHOUT THIS BOOK I have given you suggestions for Daily Affirmations that coincide with the message or theme that was being discussed that week. Some of your personal affirmations will stay the same and some of them will change at different times in your life based on what's happening or what you are hoping to achieve. For example, at the beginning of my journey one of my affirmations was: "I am learning to love myself." I still say that one, but I also say: "Every part of me is strong and beautiful." I've also changed things up a bit in the career area. At first my affirmation was, "I will write my book." Now it's changed to, "My book is successful and it helps many people."

Think long and hard about your goals and aspirations. Think about the positive thoughts you want to send out into the world. Think about the positive energy that you want to bring back to yourself, because what you put out into the world comes back to you. You know now that you are worthy and deserving.

Affirmations are a way of helping your mind to replace negative thoughts with positive ones. Repeating positive affirmations daily helps to create new pathways within your brain; which makes it easier to adopt new and empowering thoughts and beliefs. Affirmations are:

- Always specific and in present tense. *(I AM,* rather than *I WILL BE)*
- Keep them short and sweet
- Use them to build a bridge. (i.e. at first you might start with, I AM learning to love my body)
- Make sure that they coincide with your goals and values.
- Consistency is the key. Every day upon waking or just before bed.
- Make it your own. Light a candle or burning palo santo or sage.
- Write the daily affirmations on your white board or paper and post where you can see them or write them on a little card or piece of paper to carry with you and repeat throughout the day.

Write 5 of your own personal affirmations. Affirmations that coincide with the goals that you have for yourself over the next 6 months to a year. When you finish this book, post your Vision Board and your Personal Affirmations in a place where you will see them every day. Speak your affirmations out loud daily.

day 7: celebrate the new you!

TODAY'S AFFIRMATION: *I choose to be kind to myself and love myself unconditionally.*

WRITE a letter from the version of yourself who fully loves him or herself. Tell yourself how great you are, what you are going to accomplish. Talk about some of the exercises in this book that have stood out for you the most. Think about your goals and dreams and tell your inner self where you *WILL BE* based on what you *ARE* going to accomplish, because you are so amazing! Write about anything that comes to mind or that you feel your inner self needs to hear.

Sandy Lynn

Complete the following statement: I AM

who are you

WHO ARE YOU?

WRITE out all of your "I AM" statements from Week 1 to Week 13 below. Recognize the person you have become through this 90 day journey.

I AM _____

I AM _____

I AM _____

I AM _____

I AM _____

I AM _____

Sandy Lynn

I AM
___

I AM
___

I AM
___

I AM
___

I AM
___

I AM
___

I AM
___

after this book?

AFTER THIS BOOK?
ONE DAY AT A TIME, ONE STEP AT A TIME

The 5 Reiki Principles:
Just for today I will let go of anger.
Just for today I will let go of worry.
Just for today I will do my work honestly.
Just for today I will be grateful for my many blessings.
Just for today I will be kind to every living thing.

HEALING IS AN ONGOING PROCESS

FIRST OF ALL, you need to know how proud I am of you for completing this journal. You should be very proud of yourself as well. You have come such a long way, and given yourself some big **HUGS!** Healing is not an easy thing to do, and a lot of these steps that you have taken were very difficult. *Not everyone is brave enough to do what you have done*. I hope that you will continue on your journey to loving yourself, because you are an amazing and beautiful soul. Keep this journal somewhere close, so that you can look at it again and see how far you've come. Healing is an ongoing process; and as you continue to heal, I also want to remind you not to get discouraged when you hit some slumps and bumps. The path is not always a lovely little skip through the woods. Sometimes there are rocks to go around, and fallen trees to climb over and streams to cross. And sometimes you're going to want to just sit in those slumps or you might be too tired to crawl over those bumps. The *Shoulda Coulda Wouldas* and the *Yeahbuts* will creep out of their hiding places and try to take over. But I know that you are strong and you will continue to fight.

One of the most important things to remember is that not everyone is going to support you. They may not understand why you are making changes in your life. In some cases it will make them uncomfortable. It is up to you to decide which relationships serve your highest good and which ones you have to leave behind. In my case I built relationships with people that were not necessarily good for me, but being around them helped me to bury and ignore my pain, at least temporarily. I'm not going to lie, when I had to leave them behind it really hurt. That's the thing about healing. Sometimes things will feel like they are getting much worse, and in a lot of ways they will be. Sometimes it might feel like your whole world is falling apart. Think back to PART 3–Give to Yourself, when we talked about building your castle on the sand. You are in the process of rebuilding on solid ground. You have to tear down to rebuild. Take your time and do it properly, *you can't rush the process* and *you can't skip any steps.*

Just remember: no one can do this for you. You have to be willing to go through the process. As my good friend and mentor, Jay Bradley, said to me, "You have to feel it to heal it." I will never forget that. He was so right. The process of actually feeling the pain was extremely difficult and exhausting, but it has been so worth it. Yes, it's going to get overwhelming. Don't kid yourself into thinking that you can go to one or two therapy sessions or a couple of Breathwork sessions and you're going to be all good. You have to be willing to put in the work. If things seem overwhelming just break them down into smaller steps. Maybe right now you can't see yourself meditating for 15 minutes. So start with just breathing and being present for 1 minute and work your way up. It's just like working out or training for something. You're not going to start with a 5 mile run if you're not a runner. You're going to start small and work your way up to 5 miles. Recognize the steps you're taking and give yourself credit for moving forward, no matter how small you think the step is.

As I have gone through this process I have learned so much about myself. There were so many things that I was holding on to; things that I was completely unaware of that were causing me so much pain. I thought that I was working on one thing, but under that layer there were other totally different things that I needed to heal. It kind of reminds me of when you get a gift for a friend and as a gag you box it and wrap it, and then box it and wrap it again and again. As you are unwrapping the layers of healing, it seems like a long and painful process. But as you tear off each layer, the wrapping underneath is prettier and prettier and you keep going because you can't wait to get to the actual gift. In this case, each layer of healing helps your soul to shine brighter and brighter.

SUGGESTIONS AND SUCCESS STORIES

Things That Worked for Me

One of the things that I want to reinforce here is that we are all unique and beautiful souls, and what works for some people might not work for others. I'm going to take some time here to talk to you about what I have learned as I have been going through my process, and share some of the things that have worked for me. It took me a long time and a lot of exploration to find my path. My hope, and the purpose for writing this book, is that sharing my story and experiences will help you find your way. As you read through my experiences, note that I did often have some apprehension or doubts that some of these things would work for me. I'm so glad I gave it all a chance. These things may appeal to you; they may not. The important thing is that you keep trying until you discover the tools that work for you.

TIPS FOR DEALING WITH 'SLUMPS'

We all have setbacks. We all have triggers. Sometimes they'll be over quickly. Sometimes they might turn into a bad day. And sometimes we slip into a slump that we feel like we can't get out of. I'm going to share a secret with you. This is something that I haven't told anyone. I've never even said this out loud. Recently I received my copy of the video of our Vixens dance performance. I was so excited to see it and I couldn't wait to show it to my friends who couldn't make it to the show. But I haven't shown anyone. Why? Because when I brought it home and watched it, I cried. I cried because when I saw myself on the video all I concentrated on was how awful *I thought* I looked. I forgot about how wonderful the experience was. I lost the empowered woman who was proud of her body. At the same time I was also nursing a knee injury that occurred as a result of overworking during my workouts on top of the dancing so I wasn't exercising as much. I got a lot of comments from people about how it sucks getting old, and a few chuckles at the thought of me injuring myself while dancing at 55 years old. I slipped into a slump. I'm coming out the other side of it now, but I still haven't shared the video with anyone.

If you're having a setback or you slip into a slump, allow yourself the time to feel, process and let go before you try to move forward. Don't beat yourself up about it. Just keep trying until you find something that works for you. Like I've said before, we are all unique and because of this we all have different tools that will work better for us. Here are just a few suggestions:

- Journaling–Writing may help you process feelings that you are completely unaware of.
  - What is bothering you the most right now? Describe how it feels.
  - Write about your biggest fear? Why are you thinking about it so much right now?
  - There are so many things that we can't control. Make a list of things that you are worrying about that are out of your control.
- Remember to use the 90 Second Rule (from Week 4)
- Calm yourself–observe your thoughts, you are not your emotions, stay present, validate from within
- Yoga breathing–Deep Belly Breath, Alternate Nostril Breathing, Lion's Breath
- Mindful shower or mindful eating–these are great for someone who has trouble with meditation
- Make a feel-good playlist

- Meditative drawing or painting
- Butterfly Hug
- Tapping
- Repeat the Reiki Principles (Just for today…)

There are so many resources and videos online for each of the methods listed above; and so many more methods you can check out. The most important thing is to never stop trying. I didn't find Breathwork until I was 52 years old; but when I found it, it changed my life. And by the way….dance class starts again next week and I'm going to be there!

BREATHWORK–MY PERSONAL SAVING GRACE

For my entire life I have felt like something was missing, like there was something I was 'meant to do'. There was a big, empty hole in my chest and I had no idea why. And so I searched for fulfillment wherever I could find it, mostly in bad relationships, leading to some questionable life choices. Always putting myself last, always uplifting others at the cost of my own feelings. I was also raised in a family in which we were taught to internalize our emotions, which was weighing me down more than I realized and causing other physical issues in my body.

One night I was sitting on my couch….completely lost. My adult children had recently moved out to live in their own homes. I had no idea what to do with myself if I wasn't taking care of someone else. The big empty hole in my chest was back, and it dawned on me that I needed to learn to live for myself for the first time in my life. So once again I began searching for the missing piece. I happened to stumble across a Breathwork website. I felt a connection to this gentleman who lived in Los Angeles. He looked very familiar to me and after much thought I realized that he was from my hometown and we had gone to bible camp together as children. I decided to contact Jay Bradley (breatheonit.net) and get some more information about this modality.

Breathwork is a term used to refer to breathing pattern exercises that are used to improve physical, mental and/or spiritual health. The practice is conscious, which means the participant is actively involved, breathing in and out through the mouth, making it the ideal practice for those who have trouble meditating. There are many types of Breathwork, but the one I prefer is called Pranayama, a 3 part circular pattern. During a Breathwork session you will lie down in a comfortable position and then inhale into the belly, and then the chest, and exhale, all through the mouth, while music plays in the background. This practice assists in healing past wounds, both physical and emotional. It can help to change old patterns and habits, and release emotional pain and stress. As you become more deeply involved in the session, you will feel yourself releasing the pain of the physical body, and healing from the inside out.

My first Breathwork session was uncomfortable at first, but it was also life altering. Initially I struggled with the idea of releasing my feelings and allowing myself to be vulnerable. I also had a very hard time telling myself "I love you." But as I allowed myself to just sink into the rhythm of the breathing I was able to let go. I released pain and trauma that I had been carrying for my entire life. I unloaded guilt that I wasn't even aware that I was carrying. And as I worked through the next few sessions, I finally learned to love myself. My outlook on life was so much more positive as I was living in a positive energy. As I continued with this practice and completed more sessions, Breathwork literally rewired my brain and shifted my energy to a more positive outlook filled with peace and gratitude. It benefited me physically, as well as mentally and spiritually.

As I studied more and more about Breathwork and trained under Jay Bradley, I realized that I had finally found my missing piece. I was meant to be a healer. I had, in a sense, been doing it all my life, but now I had found the tool that I wanted to use to make a difference. My fulfillment comes from assisting others to heal themselves and to transform to a place of self love and happiness. I am constantly receiving feedback from clients about how much Breathwork has helped them through things like trauma and anxiety and brought them to a place of self-acceptance. Since I started this journey I have progressed from being a Breathwork practitioner, to creating and presenting workshops on self-love, to now completing my dream of writing this book! And that's just the tip of the iceberg!

So…when I tell you that Breathwork can and will change your life, I am speaking from a place of experience; and my mission is to bring that experience to as many people as I possibly can!

For more information on Breathwork and testimonials from my clients please visit my website at breathehealingcentre.com

PUSH YOURSELF OUT OF YOUR COMFORT ZONE ….YOU MAY REALIZE THAT YOU'RE NOT ALONE!

When it comes to stepping outside your comfort zone, you can do this with baby steps if you need to. Every little step counts. The first step for me just happened to be signing up for a dance program. I wrote earlier about my apprehension when I took the Vixens dance classes. I really wanted to do it, but I was so nervous about it. The interesting thing is that when the class was winding up I told all of the women about the book I was writing and I asked them if they would be willing to contribute by sharing some of their feelings during this experience. I was so surprised when I read their responses. This was a group of women that ranged from their early 20's to their mid 60's. Even the women that came across to me as gorgeous and self-confident had a lot of fear and anxiety about taking this class and putting themselves out there. So never feel like you're alone or you're the only one that has anxiety about stepping out of your box. By the end of the program, these women, like me, felt it was a beautiful and empowering experience and they were so glad they had done it:

- "I signed up because I love how dance makes me feel free and gets me out of my head and I wanted to feel a part of a community. On the first day I was a bit nervous but more curious and anxious/excited. I wanted to cry when stepping on that stage again as it makes me feel so alive and happy and is one of the places where I truly feel myself."

- "It's hard to explain in just a few words. Being part of VIXENS generally, and being part of my group specifically, brought me a sense of community that I don't feel here. I felt accepted, encouraged, supported, valued, wanted, inspired, and safe. It nudged me out of my comfort zone, helped me reconnect to my postpartum body, and gave me a creative goal to work toward. I am excited that I was able to be part of the beginning of something big."

- "I tend to go into group settings feeling very alone, isolated, and independent. It can be difficult to make friends in adulthood because everyone seems like they're already paired up, and sometimes it feels like there's no room for the new kid. Another thing I struggled with was seeing my body in the full length wall of mirrors - I don't generally struggle with this, but I currently feel like I don't recognize my postpartum body as mine. It can be disorienting to look at yourself but not see yourself. Having that constant visual exposure, as well as seeing the progress of our choreography really helped me reorient myself."

I Am...

I definitely can't talk about Vixens without mentioning the woman behind this amazing program, Jessi McCulloch, co-owner of Renegade Performing Arts in Thunder Bay, Ontario, Canada. She started out as my dance teacher, but I am now so proud to call her a mentor and a friend. I told her about this book and asked if I could share some of her thoughts, and I am so thankful that she agreed.

When I asked her what brought her to start the Vixens program, a lot of what she said really resonated with me. She said first: "I was raised to not like other women. I was told that other women are a threat. Don't be friends, don't lift each other up. As I've gotten older I've seen that that's just so fucked. There's misogyny in everything, not just men. There's misogynistic women as well." As she was on her own healing journey, she came to a place where she began to question the views she grew up with. She wanted to do something to break the cycle within herself and other women as well. She believes that it's important that women realize that they can be more than one thing. "It doesn't have to be like you're just a mom, you're just this, you're just that. You're not allowed to be sexy once you hit this age." She wanted to create a program that was about community and 'finding your sexy'.

For about 10 years now, Renegade Performing Arts has been putting on a show called Le Cabaret Noir. Jessi says she knew that there was a need for and an interest in 'burlesque' ish dance programs, because there were people who expressed interest in joining Le Cabaret Noir but maybe weren't at that level yet performance wise or skill wise. Vixens was a way to make it accessible to all ages, skills and performance levels. For Jessi, Vixens is about taking power over your own body and your own sexuality, whatever that means to you. Her motto is: "Tits up! Ass out!" I can personally attest to the fact that this is so empowering, especially doing it with a whole group of women. This creates a community where everybody is beautiful no matter their age, race, or size. "Everybody has their own thing that makes them beautiful and I love being able to help people find what that is." One of the biggest rewards for her is seeing the difference in her students' confidence levels from day one to performance day.

I asked Jessi if she felt like she had accomplished her goal with the Vixens program:

Holy shit! Did I ever! The night of the final performance I was so proud and grateful. I was beside the stage telling myself, 'suck it up, no tears, you have eyelashes on!" Even through all of the stress of putting on the show I was just beaming! People were coming up to me after the show just crying after seeing their loved ones perform saying how far they've come confidence wise and how it's poured into every aspect of their life because of this program. The whole next day after the Vixens show I cried all day. I went for a run and I will never forget this moment. I suddenly started sprinting, thinking about how far I have come in the past couple of years personally, mentally, emotionally, physically and then I started thinking about how cool it was to empower 35 women and how we sold out the club. I didn't even know if anybody would come to the show but we sold out NV. The positive feedback was wild! Even if people thought 'well it's not something I would do', they still said that it was the coolest thing ever to watch. All of these women up there being confident, being who they are, breaking all the boundaries and the stereotypes. Yes, I'm the teacher but it's also all of the people that are in it, like we all create the environment together. So I'm thinking about this and I'm running and suddenly I'm just fucking sprinting and I'm bawling and bawling and I'm laughing and I'm bawling. I was like "I can't believe this is my life. This is so cool. This is the coolest thing ever!" I am just so, so grateful and I feel so lucky.

Jessi, you are an inspiration. You talked about your reasons for starting Vixens Heels Dance Performance Program at the open house. Anybody can talk, but you actually meant every word that you said. Your encouragement and support, your belief in what you are doing and, in your students, has more of an impact on women like me than I think you will ever know. This program, I am sure, has done so much for so many women. The world needs more people like you and more programs like this. I am so honored to have met you as I am on this journey to not only self love but encouraging other women to love themselves.

start your story

"The privilege of a lifetime is to become who you truly are."
Carl Jung

WE HAVE COME to the end of this journey, and I hope you have enjoyed the trip. I know that I have healed and grown while writing it, and I hope that it has done the same for you. I would just like to share a few last words with you now and ask you this question: What do you want your story to be?

Before you answer that, think about the books that you have read or stories you have been told. Have you ever found yourself becoming completely immersed in the words, feeling as if you were actually living it? Like in J.K. Rowling's Harry Potter books, where you could envision Hogwarts and Diagon Alley and imagine yourself right there with all of the characters. As a reader you actually feel and experience the joy, the fear, the sorrow and the anticipation right along with the characters. A good storyteller takes control of the story and decides how they want to tell it based on the way they want the audience to feel.

Now let's relate this to life. We all have stories. Some stories are happy; full of joy and memories that make you smile. Some stories are sad; full of trauma and heartbreak. No matter what kind of story you have, take a minute to think about the way you tell it to other people. Are you wanting them to be sad or happy when they hear your story? Are you wanting them to feel sorry for you, be amazed by you, comment on how strong you are? Remember that the way that you tell your story is going to affect the way that they see you and the way they feel while spending time with you. Now let's switch gears again and think about the way you tell your story….to yourself. Are you the hero or the victim? Do you spend more time in the happy parts or the sad parts? What is the main theme of your story?

My point is…one of the first steps to healing is realizing that you are the author of your own story. Maybe you can't control everything that happens in your story, but you can control how you react to it. There's that famous line from the movie Forest Gump where Forest says, "Mama says life is like a box of chocolates, you never know what you're gonna get." It's a great line, but you know what I say? If you want a better idea of what you're going to get, stop letting somebody else make your damn chocolates!

I spent many years allowing the heartaches and hardships of my life to control who I was and how I viewed myself. I was letting other people narrate my story. I was letting the words and actions of other people tell me my worth, the way I should be treated, and what my path should be; and the funny thing was, I didn't even realize it. And then one day I was sitting alone in my living room. I was single, my children had moved into their own homes, and I had no idea what to do with myself. I had no one to take care of, no one to tell me what they needed me to do. I had this revelation that all of my life I had been existing…not living.

It was time for me to take the scariest step of my life and take back my story.

I'm not going to lie, it wasn't easy, and some days it's still a struggle. Thankfully I stumbled upon Jay Bradley and Breathwork and that helped to rewire my brain. I had to learn to tell myself that I was worth it, that I deserved to live my life the way I wanted to. I had to learn that it's ok to be selfish sometimes and do what's best for me. I had to learn to change my thinking and try to find the positive in each day, sometimes each moment.

Slowly I began to take my story back, ending the negative chapters and leaving those events and characters behind, and folding the corners of the pages that made me smile so that I could revisit them when I needed to. Healing is an ongoing process; I work at it every day. I continue to write my story my way. And I choose to share my experience with others and feel blessed when I can be a part of their healing journey. If you choose to remember anything from my story, let it be this:

It doesn't matter if you have to start over, as long as you start. It doesn't matter how small the step is, as long as you take it. It doesn't matter what happened last week, yesterday, or even one minute ago, because at any given moment you can take a deep breath and tell yourself:

"MY STORY STARTS RIGHT NOW!"

Much love, Sandy

recommended resources

BOOKS:

- Atlas of the Heart–Brene Brown
- The 4 Agreements–Don Miguel Ruiz
- Letting Go–David Hawkins
- Whole Brain Living–Dr. Jill Bolte Taylor
- Live Look Feel: The 12-Week Guide to Live Longer, Look Younger & Feel Better!--Jay Bradley
- Channeled Writing Journal: Access the Thoughts of Your Soul–Ellie Shoja

Videos:

- My Stroke of Insight (Ted Talk)

For more information on Breathwork, the book, or my talks and workshops please visit my website: www.breathehealingcentre.com

references

BATES, J. (2020, May 13). *"letting go" by David Hawkins: The book that shifted my entire reality.* Jordan Bates. https://jordanbates.life/letting-go-david-hawkins/

Holland, K. (2019, June 12). *Average waist size for women: Measurements, ratios, and more.* Healthline. https://www.healthline.com/health/average-waist-size-for-women

Revealing average screen time statistics for 2025. Backlinko. (2025, January 31). https://backlinko.com/screen-time-statistics

Ruiz, D. M. (1997). *The four agreements: A Practical Guide to Personal Freedom.* Amber-Allen Pub.

Solan, M. (2021, November 1). *Health and happiness go hand in hand.* Harvard Health. https://www.health.harvard.edu/mind-and-mood/health-and-happiness-go-hand-in-hand#:~:text=Research%20suggests%20that%2C%20on%20average%2C%2050%25%20of%20people%E2%80%99s,and%20the%20remaining%2010%25%20depends%20on%20the%20circumstances.

Team, S. (2023, May 13). *20 self esteem statistics that will help you feel better (2025)*. https://www.soocial.com/self-esteem-statistics/

"Do you love Me?" Alice asked.
"No, I don't love you!" replied the White Rabbit.
Alice frowned and clasped her hands together as she did whenever she felt hurt.
"See?" replied the White Rabbit. "Now you're going to start asking yourself what makes you so imperfect and what did you do wrong so that I can't love you at least a little.
You know, that's why I can't love you. You will not always be loved, Alice, there will be days when others will be tired and bored with life, will have their heads in the clouds, and will hurt you.
Because people are like that, they somehow always end up hurting each other's feelings, whether through carelessness, misunderstanding, or conflicts with themselves.
If you don't love yourself, at least a little, if you don't create an armor of self-love and happiness around your heart, the feeble annoyances caused by others will become lethal and will destroy you.
The first time I saw you I made a pact with myself: 'I will avoid loving you until you learn to love yourself.' "

~Misattributed to Lewis Carroll, Alice in Wonderland but Author Unknown

about the author

Sandy Lynn is a college professor, former educational administrator and mother who was born and raised in Northwestern Ontario, Canada. Sandy knows first-hand about the long-term effects of childhood trauma, domestic abuse, and an overall lack of self love.

After beginning her healing journey several years ago, and experimenting with many different modalities, she discovered the amazing benefits of Breathwork and Reiki. After studying to become a practitioner of both, she stepped away from full time administration in order to focus on combining her healing expertise and life experiences to help others fall in love with themselves. She now dedicates most of her time to writing, speaking and facilitating self-love workshops.

- instagram.com/sandylynn_breathehealingcentre
- facebook.com/sandylynn.breathehealingcentre
- tiktok.com/@sandylynn0530